After the Gold Rush
A sustainable Olympics for London

Edited by Anthony Vigor,
Melissa Mean and Charlie Tims

The Institute for Public Policy Research (ippr) is the UK's leading progressive think tank and was established in 1988. Its role is to bridge the political divide between the social democratic and liberal traditions, the intellectual divide between academia and the policy making establishment and the cultural divide between government and civil society. It is first and foremost a research institute, aiming to provide innovative and credible policy solutions. Its work, the questions its research poses and the methods it uses are driven by the belief that the journey to a good society is one that places social justice, democratic participation and economic and environmental sustainability at its core.

For further information you can contact ippr's external affairs department on info@ippr.org, you can view our website at www.ippr.org and you can buy our books from Central Books on 0845 458 9910 or email ippr@centralbooks.com.

DEM⊙S

Demos is a greenhouse for new ideas which can improve the quality of our lives. As an independent think tank, we aim to create an open resource of knowledge and learning that operates beyond traditional party politics.

We connect researchers, thinkers and practitioners to an international network of people changing politics. Our ideas regularly influence government policy, but we also work with companies, NGOs, colleges and professional bodies.

You can contact us at: Demos, Third Floor, Magdalen House, 136 Tooley Street, London SE1 2TU, tel: 0845 458 5949, www.demos.co.uk.

ISBN 1 86030 260 2

Production and design by Emphasis Midlands
Cover design by Hoop Associates
Printed and bound by HenDi Systems

Acknowledgements

The Institute for Public Policy Research (ippr) and Demos would like to thank our project partners and sponsors. Without their willingness to contribute to our research this project could not have happened. Our thanks go to: British Waterways; Camelot Group Plc; the Environment Agency; the Greater London Authority and Sport England.

The findings of our research are, however, the responsibility of the authors alone and do not necessarily represent the views of our funding partners or any other individual or organisation involved in the project.

We would like to thank all those individuals who have contributed to the ideas contained in this report. In particular: Nick Bent (DCMS); Syrus Bittaali (London Development Agency); Richard Brown (Greater London Authority); Beth Fowler (Sport England); Ed Fox (British Waterways); Pam Gilder (Environment Agency); Dan Hawthorn (Greater London Authority); Stephen Jacobs (London 2012); Debbie Jevans (London 2012); Jude Kelly (Metal and London 2012); Sarah Kennedy (Camelot Group plc); Nick Rowe (Sport England); Richard Rutter (British Waterways); David Stubbs (London 2012); John Zerafa (London 2012). We would also like to thanks the individual chapter authors for their patience and good nature in responding to our editorial deadlines and advice.

Our thanks also goes to the people that gave their time to attend the seminars – for providing both fuel for lively discussion and ideas for us to reflect on.

Finally, we would also like to thank the following individuals from within ippr and Demos: Tom Bentley, Kate Carey, Richard Darlington, Louise Every, Eddie Gibb, Tim Gibbs, Tony Grayling, Chris Moss, Nick Pearce, Nathan Sansom and James Wilsdon. Matt Jackson deserves particular thanks.

All of these people, and many more, made invaluable contributions; any omissions and errors remain our own.

Anthony Vigor, Melissa Mean and Charlie Tims
October 2004

Foreword

This summer, we've seen the transforming effect of hosting the Olympics. Athens is a changed place: cleaner, brighter, easier to get around, vibrant and modern. Now the Games are over it will be interesting to see what the legacy of 2004 will mean for Athens and for Greece. Whatever the lasting impact, it is clear that it isn't simply the sixty days of sporting competition and cultural festivals that change a city. In Athens, as with Barcelona in 1992, the Olympics was a catalyst for investment and the Games themselves an opportunity to present the city and country in a new light.

I welcome this ippr/Demos report on what winning the 2012 bid could mean for London and the UK. We need to have a public debate about what we want the Olympics and Paralympics to bring to Britain, because it will only be by working together – businesses, local authorities, government, charities and individuals – that we will maximise the benefits of bringing the Games to Britain. This collection of essays illustrates the challenges of creating an Olympic Games that leaves a positive legacy.

As the report concludes we have to be realistic about what we can achieve through hosting the Games, but that doesn't mean we can't be ambitious. With the right strategies in place, we can use the experience of hosting the Olympics to deliver a qualitative change in the quality of life for people in East London – creating the largest new urban park in Europe for two hundred years, providing new housing, new community sporting facilities, a cleaner, safer place to live. And the impact of the Games won't stop with London. We can use the enthusiasm generated by the Olympics and Paralympics to help us get the population more active, to get people more engaged with their communities, to improve sporting facilities across the UK. But it won't happen unless we have specific strategies in place.

I am pleased to see that some of the challenges and risks identified in this report are those we have already begun to factor into our plans. It is particularly important to understand the message that only by embedding legacy planning into every aspect of our preparations for the Games will we make the most the opportunities available to us. Legacy matters to the IOC; the Olympics, if they are to continue to flourish, have to be affordable and to bring clear benefits to the host city and nation. More than ever before, the cities bidding for the 2012 Games have to provide evidence of the legacy plans for every facility that they plan to create and assess the broad impact that hosting the Games will have.

I am confident that the proposals we submit to the IOC in November will reassure the IOC that we have put legacy planning at the heart of our bid, and give us the best possible chance of winning the vote in Singapore next year.

Tessa Jowell
Secretary of State for Culture Media and Sport

About the authors

Fred Coalter is Professor of Sports Policy at the University of Stirling. Previously he was the Director of the Centre for Leisure Research at the University of Edinburgh. Recent work includes *The Role of Sport in Regenerating Deprived Urban Areas* (Scottish Executive), *Realising the Potential of Cultural Services* (Local Government Association) and *Sport and Community Development: a manual* (**sport**scotland). He has been a member of several committees and working groups including, the Council of Europe's Working Group on Sport and Social Exclusion, the Sports Advisory Board of the Neighbourhood Renewal Unit in the Office of the Deputy Prime Minister and Sport England's Working Group on Performance Measurement for the Development of Sport. He is also Chair of Edinburgh Leisure Ltd (the trust which manages sports provision for the City of Edinburgh Council) and a member of the editorial board of Managing Leisure: an international journal.

Martin Crookston is a Director of Llewelyn Davies, responsible for the firm's economic and policy work. He is an economist and urban/regional planner with thirty years of experience in managing complex research and development projects for a wide range of corporate and public sector bodies both in Britain and overseas. For over a decade, he has been working on the development challenges of the Thames Gateway sub-region to the east of London. He also led the *Socio-Economic Assessment of London* study carried out for the Association of London Government, and has directed and contributed to major studies in many cities and regions both in Britain and overseas including the 1996 Four World Cities comparative economic and policy study of London, Paris, New York and Tokyo, with Professor Sir Peter Hall and Comedia, for the Government Office for London.

Keith Khan was recently appointed as the chief executive of The Rich Mix Centre in Bethnal Green, East London. The centre, due to open in 2005, aims to become a place of exchange between different art forms, communities and cultural traditions. Keith is an award-winning artist who is trained in sculpture, loves carnival and is preoccupied with internationalism, culture and identity. He was Director of Design for the opening and closing ceremonies of the Commonwealth Games 2002 and Artistic Director of Celebration Commonwealth, for the Queen's Jubilee Parade in Central London, June 2002. In 1990 Keith Khan and Ali Zaidi founded the London-based firm Motiroti. The company is led by a group of artists who make use of a wide range of artistic practices, such as photography, architecture, new technology, performance and film.

Roger Levett is a consultant specialising in sustainability policy, management and monitoring. He is the main author of *A Better Choice of Choice* (Fabian Society, 2003) and is helping edit the forthcoming Club of Rome report *Limits to Privatisation*. He wrote *Towards the Ecopolis* with Ian Christie for the acclaimed Demos/Comedia *Richness of Cities* series.

Melissa Mean is a Senior Researcher at Demos, where she leads 'The Next City', Demos's urban programme. Previous to joining Demos, Melissa was Government Affairs Officer for the RSPB, Europe's largest environmental NGO, where she worked on climate change, transport and urban policy. Melissa has also worked for *Public Citizen* in Washington DC on environmental justice and consumer rights issues. In her spare time, Melissa is an elected board member of a community regeneration trust in Waterloo which overseas a £5million programme aimed at community development and physical renewal of the area.

Mike Raco is Lecturer in Economic Geography in the Department of Geography, University of Reading. He has published widely on the topics of urban policy, community mobilisation and the governance of economic development. In 2003 he co-edited *Urban Renaissance? New Labour, community and urban policy* (with Rob Imrie, Policy Press). Although his doctoral subject was geography, his background also includes planning and urban studies. He is currently a principal investigator on the multi-disciplinary SUBR:IM (Sustainable Urban Brownfield Regeneration: Integrated Management) research consortium examining best practice in sustainable urban regeneration in the UK.

Charlie Tims is a Researcher at Demos, where his interests include the public realm, creativity, culture and identity issues. He has worked with a variety stakeholders in the public and private sectors to develop new ways of expressing the value of heritage and culture in education and social enterprise. He is currently involved in developing new approaches to understanding public space and its place in urban policy. He holds a first class degree in Modern History from the University of St Andrews.

Anthony Vigor is a Research Fellow within the sustainability team at the Institute for Public Policy Research (ippr). He joined ippr from the University of Manchester where he completed a PhD in the politics of regional economic development within the UK and US. He is particularly interested in regional policy, economic development, urban regeneration, sports policy and community development and has published articles in *The New Statesman, New Economy, The Municipal Journal* and *Local Economy*. Whilst at ippr, Anthony has co-authored *A New Regional Policy for the UK* and worked extensively on the opening of a new ippr office within the North East. He is also an Honorary Research Fellow at the University of Manchester.

Executive Summary

Introduction

The Olympic Games generates lots of enthusiasm and great expectations. More than simply a sporting event, hosting 'the greatest show on earth' is seen by some as a 'once in a lifetime opportunity' to provide new infrastructure and deliver benefits to local residents and communities. Those organising the London 2012 Bid are no different, claiming a Games would deliver a legacy of new sporting facilities, thousands of new jobs, new businesses, a 'step-change' in the nation's physical activity and ultimately a transformation of the East End of London.

But an analysis of past Olympic Games reveals that there is no guaranteed beneficial legacy from hosting an Olympic Games. While the cost of hosting a Games is significant – currently estimated at £3.6 billion for London – this is only a relatively small proportion of London's annual GDP (currently around £162 billion). And there is little evidence that past Games have delivered benefits to those people and places most in need. What is clear is that those cities that have benefited most – and Barcelona is the clearest example – have entrenched the Olympics within a broader urban strategy. The challenge for London is, therefore, to embed the preparation for and hosting of the Games into a broader social policy agenda from the outset. Given the levels of disadvantage in the East End of London, this is especially important.

A sustainable social legacy

There will be a significant amount of new development in the Lower Lea Valley whether London hosts the 2012 Olympic Games or not. This does provide the opportunity for a significant amount of regeneration, but the detail must be right. In the past flagship regeneration projects have tended to prioritise change as a good in itself, with development *in* the area taking place rather than development *of* the area.

Games-related development must be embedded within existing projects, agencies and partnerships and could provide an opportunity to bring additional resources into the area. Securing such local involvement early on will be key; delivering a sustainable social legacy will require significant involvement from the bottom-up, and too often in the past the social legacy has been an afterthought. Another fundamental part of this process must be the setting of realistic ambitions, around which some debate is encouraged. If these issues are addressed, a London 2012 Olympic Games and the redevelopment of the Lower Lea Valley provide the opportunity to develop a model of best practice for regeneration.

A sustainable employment legacy

A London 2012 Olympic Games will offer an opportunity to provide employment benefits, but this will require significant planning from the outset to achieve. Despite being the UK's most prosperous region, London has a low employment rate, with East London suffering from particularly low rates. The employment problem is not due to a lack of available employment, but rather due to significant 'supply-side' problems (for example, low skills and employer hiring practices).

If Games-related development is to provide new employment opportunities to those who are currently unemployed, then detailed work is required with both employers and potential employees. The employment opportunities must be identified, employers' recruitment techniques need to be better understood and individuals, often with low skills, need to be readied so they can access these opportunities. Without such proactive measures there is a real danger that any new employment opportunities will solely be accessed by well qualified individuals travelling from across the South East.

A sustainable environmental legacy

The IOC's stated aim is that hosting an Olympic Games should have no negative net impact on the environment. No previous Games has met this tough challenge – not even the so-called 'green games' in Sydney. It is a challenge that London could and should make its own

– adding both to the distinctiveness of its Olympic Bid and its legacy value. London should adopt the twin principles of avoiding/reducing negative environmental impacts and where this is not possible, off-setting them with an appropriate environmental benefit. A sustainable environmental legacy for London's Games also needs to go beyond the minimum of a one-off greening of the Olympic site and facilities. Instead, it must help boost capacity to start closing the gap between environmental targets and actually delivering on them across the whole of the UK. This challenge is less a technical one and more a matter of breaking through cultural and institutional inertia. This will require a proactive, interventionist, public interest-driven delivery process and a strong emphasis on developing the market for green technology.

A sustainable sporting legacy

For a London 2012 Olympics to deliver a sustainable sporting legacy it must contribute towards an increase in sports participation across the UK. Past host cities have tended to expect the Olympics to automati-cally deliver this. However, the evidence shows that past Olympics have failed to bring with them a sustained increase in participation. To avoid a similar mistaken expectation, a London 2012 Olympics must only be one element of the broader sports participation agenda.

The challenge will be to convert the increased interest that an Olympics would bring into sustained participation. To achieve this, a 2012 London Olympics must focus attention on grassroots sports. A partnership approach will also be an imperative as schools, clubs and sport agencies work effectively together. And fundamentally, an imag-inative and proactive approach is required to capitalise on any inter-est as soon as possible.

A sustainable cultural legacy

If a London 2012 Olympics is to realise the IOC's aspiration to place culture and education on an equal footing to sport then it will have to go beyond simply using culture as a marketing tool. A sustainable cultural legacy would represent an opportunity to build lasting links amongst a disparate cultural sector and foster new forms of partnership working with schools, organisations and individuals throughout the UK and overseas. If this is to be achieved, the whole of the sector will need to be engaged, including its disruptive fringes.

The combination of culture and the Olympics represents a chance to learn and investigate ourselves as a nation, rather than just presenting a summary in an opening ceremony. If this is to be lasting, the use of cultural programming in the Games will have to contribute directly towards widening access to culture and participation in it and in so doing increase our ability to better understand ourselves and one another. Only if this is achieved could the Games be considered 'culturally sustainable'.

A sustainable London Olympics

To secure a sustainable legacy, the challenge is to minimise the frequent mismatch between the infrastructure and investment required to run a successful Games and the longer term needs of the host community. To achieve this will require a proactive approach. It is clear that a significant element of a sustainable legacy will be secured before the Games themselves. In doing this, three organising principles will be fundamental.

First, the Olympics must be embedded within existing mainstream programmes and policy agendas that start well before 2012 and continue well after. There are policies, programmes and initiatives at all scales of government that are relevant and provide opportunities. Second, the Olympics uniquely mobilises people, interest and resources. There is an opportunity to strategically use this 'Olympics effect' to suspend some elements of 'business as usual' and deliver higher environmental quality, sports participation rates and levels of volunteering. Thirdly, for local communities to fully benefit from any opportunities, there must be an investment in community capacity and ownership.

The nine policies ideas outlined below aim to contribute towards securing a sustainable legacy. They do not represent a wish list and are careful not to make unrealistic claims on public finances – indeed some are designed to generate extra resources. Overall however, there must also be a recognition that to deliver a sustainable Olympics long-term spending must not only be on hard infrastructure (for example, new facilities) but also softer social infrastructure. As one of our interviewees put it: 'Delivering the legacy will be a people issue. Do not for one minute think it will only be facilities issue.'

Our proposals are:

- Community Enterprise Endowment Fund

- Off-Setting Programme

- Employment Taskforce

- The Street Olympics

- Codifying a Healthy City

- International Olympic Corps

- Volunteer Programme Plus

- An Annual National School Olympics

- A Cultural Resource for Open Learning

1 **Introduction**

Anthony Vigor,
Melissa Mean and
Charlie Tims

1 Introduction

Anthony Vigor, Melissa Mean and Charlie Tims

On 25 July 1992 in the darkened Barcelona stadium Paralympic archer Antonio Rebollo lit the end of an arrow from the Olympic torch and took aim. The blazing arrow curved high in the sky, then dipped to hit the cauldron, igniting the Olympic Flame that would preside over the twenty nine days of sport. Or did it? Those in the know claim the arrow missed its target and sailed off into the distance. Only TV cameras placed at just the right angle made the magic work for the two billion viewers around the globe who witnessed the opening ceremony.

As in the BBC's ad campaign for its coverage of this year's Athens Games, the Olympics[1] can make and remake legends. They are also quite good at myth-making and when thinking about the potential legacy of a Games, it is wise to be wary of this. The long-term impact of a Games is frequently a matter of debate and controversy. Caution needs to be exercised in accepting all that is claimed. These claims usually centre on the positive infrastructure side effects of staging a Games and the benefits from a surge in tourism. However infrastructure investments are often misplaced and the benefits fail to flow back to the people and places that need them most. Equally, the flow of new tourists tends to dry up fast. Or, as Athens found, fails to appear in anything like the numbers predicted. The challenge for London is to create an architecture for a Games that is on target for delivering the mandated twenty nine days of sporting spectacle, but also connects and nourishes the long-term needs and aspirations of the communities that are playing host. It comes down to a fundamental question at the heart of the Olympic Movement – who gets to share the Olympic dream and can that share be more substantive than a trick of television?

Brand value

⚠ The five Olympic rings are the most famous brand in the world, with a recognition rate of over ninety per cent that Shell, McDonalds and even Coca-Cola envy. But what do people think when they see the rings, what is the content of the Olympic brand? The International Olympic Committee (IOC), the organisation responsible for franchising the Games to host cities, is clear about what it thinks the Olympic brand means and sets it down at the beginning of its weighty 108 page Charter:

> The goal of Olympism is to place everywhere sport at the service of the harmonious development of man, with a view to encouraging the establishment of a peaceful society concerned with the preservation of human dignity (IOC 2003).

The content and tone is very much a reflection of the time of the birth of the modern Olympics in the second half of the nineteenth century. Following several national Olympic Games in Greece, Baron De Coubertin masterminded the first international, recognisable modern Games in 1896. Against the backdrop of rising nationalist tensions in many parts of the world, De Coubertin drew heavily on the philosophy of the Enlightenment believing that sport could produce a more rational state of affairs through promoting individual and collective endeavor in an internationalist framework. Echoing ancient Greece, where the Games had been created to bring a temporary halt to the fighting between rival factions, the revived Games were seen as a way of diffusing tension between nations. The second formative influence on the modern Games was the reformist agenda of the time that sought social improvement through education. Sport, open to all, with equal participation was a more radical proposition than it might first appear. At the end of the nineteenth century sport was viewed as a leisure activity and the preserve of those sufficiently wealthy enough to participate. To use sport instead as a tool to promote social mobility marked a radical shift in thinking (Briggs, McCarthy and Zorbas 2004).

Over the 108 years and twenty-eight Summer Game
the Olympics has evolved considerably. The numb
impressive: in 1896, 311 athletes competed from thir
in the Sydney 2000 Games 10,651 athletes competed from 1˞˞
tries, watched by a global television audience of approximately 3.7
billion people. But it is more than a simple numbers game. Some of
the individual cities hosting the Games have also contributed and
extended the Olympic brand through the distinctive way in which
they have run their Games and the objectives or values they have
sought to promote. This has sometimes had positive implications for
the Olympic brand, at other times negative. The image that stuck
from Los Angeles in 1984 and Atlanta in 1996 was that of the
Olympics as a moneymaking machine for big business: LA was
dubbed the 'capitalist Games' and Atlanta the 'Coca-Cola Games'.
While the IOC has itself actively developed the commercial foundations of the Games, for example through cutting blue-chip sponsorship deals and tough bargaining over broadcasting rights, it judged
that Atlanta had tipped the balance too far and declared the IOC
would never again accept an entirely corporately funded bid from a
potential host city.

More positively, over the past twenty years the Olympics brand
has been extended to include both a green and a regeneration dimension. This additional brand value has depended on the innovative
style and strategy of two host cities: Barcelona and Sydney. Lessons
from both of these Games will be picked up later, but in the mean-
time the 2000 Sydney Games represents an important shift in the
Olympic approach worthy of comment.

Sydney 2000 is widely known as the 'green games' and is credited
with pioneering the (at the time) relatively new planning concept of
sustainable development (Chalkley and Essex 1999a). Prior to
Sydney the environmental content in preparing and running a
Games consisted of land-use, landscape and amenity considerations,
a kind of beautification of the host city rather than 'greening' it. Seoul
perhaps most starkly reflected this practice – creating hundreds of
new parks across the city was part and parcel of the same project that

...so built walls along the route of the marathon to conceal the slum housing from runners and TV cameras alike. Sydney went beyond beautification, championing ecological sustainability including biodiversity protection and enhancement and conserving natural resources such as water and energy. Its greenness was encoded in ninety principles developed by its Organising Committee's own Environmental Committee, with input from a number of campaign groups including Greenpeace. In the end, Greenpeace only awarded Sydney a begrudging bronze medal for their efforts. However, in the eyes of the press, promoters and the IOC, Sydney had bought the environment to the heart of the Olympics Movement and every bidding city since has made sure environmental value is a core part of its submission.

In many ways Sydney was an unlikely contender for delivering a green Games. At the international level, the Australian government has a well-earned roguish reputation for failing to sign up to environmental agreements including the Kyoto climate change agreement. Neither can Sydney claim to be the originator of the Olympic urge to go green. What Sydney did do very well however was read signals and signs from the IOC about what kind of Games it wanted and then had the confidence to push it a bit further. The IOC and the world of sport were slow to engage with the rise in concern over the environment which had begun in the 1970s. However, early in the 1990s sport began to catch on to environmental concerns, including the IOC who began to view care for the environment as a natural extension of its commitment to well-being of young people. In 1995 this was formalised into the Olympic Charter with the environment declared the third pillar of the Olympic Movement alongside sport and culture. Sydney won the competition to host the 2000 Games in 1993. Significantly this was before this formal change in the IOC's Charter. However, by anticipating the mood and emerging priorities of the IOC, Sydney managed to get ahead of the pack and when the IOC announced its decision it praised Sydney for its emphasis on environmental protection and its close collaboration with environmental groups.

The lessons from Sydney's story for London lie in the fact that the IOC has begun to signal that legacy matters to the Olympic brand. In 2002, the IOC changed its Charter once again to include the idea that a Games should bequeath a tangible legacy to host cities. To any outside observer, the idea that a city should embark on a project that the IOC estimates at some US$2 billion on running costs and an additional US$1 billion on infrastructure without thinking about leveraging some long term gains for the host city sounds absurd. However, currently the IOC's use of legacy is an essentially negative one, driven by a fear that the Olympics has become synonymous with gigantism, excess and expensive venues that struggle to find a use once the Olympic circus has left town. For all the triumph of Sydney as the 'best games ever', the main stadium at Homebush Bay struggles to find a use for more than once or twice a year and it remains estranged from the rest of the city. The IOC's negative definition of legacy is reflected in what is the main depository for its thinking so far on legacy, the Prague Report produced in 2003 (Olympic Games Study Commission 2003). Its 119 recommendations are exclusively concerned with cutting costs, reducing the Games' size and avoiding white elephants.

The bidding round for the right to host the 2012 Games is the first since the Charter change in 2002 and what the IOC describes as 'a fundamental change of philosophy' (Olympic Games Study Commission 2003). All the shortlisted cities have got the message about the need for a compact Games. However, the real opportunity for London to distinguish itself lies in setting out a coherent and imaginative plan for how spending an estimated £3.6 billion[2] on a sporting spectacle can have a tangible and quantifiable positive legacy for the host city, and more widely. It lies in going back to the Olympic founding values about sport being at the service of the harmonious development of humankind, interrogating these values for their contemporary meaning and setting out ways that they can be materially supported and furthered in very practical ways. To do so would be to perform an even greater trick than Sydney's of moving the Olympic brand from beautification to environmentalism; London has the opportunity to transform the prevalent negative mantra of 'no white elephants', into a positive one of meaningful, sustainable legacy.

What do we mean by sustainable legacy?

As the size of bill for putting on the Games grows, the words 'sustainable' and 'legacy' are increasingly being muttered by representatives of the IOC, bidding committees and government officials. But 'sustainable legacy' is a slippery term subject to different interpretations and diverse perspectives as to what type of legacy is desirable or achievable. Business, government (local, regional and national), community groups, residents, environmental organisations and the Olympic Movement itself all have a view, and many are actively telling their own story about what a London Games in 2012 could mean for them. All of these stories potentially entail long lasting legacies, but each has a different impact on the ground.

Competing legacy agendas
International Olympic Committee: a debt free Games
Baron de Courbertin first raised his worries over the growing size of the Games in his *Olympic Review* of 1911.

> It would be very unfortunate, if the often exaggerated expenses incurred for the most recent Olympiads . . . were to deter (small) countries from putting themselves forward to host the Olympic Games in the future (cited in Olympic Games Study Commission 2003).

The problem now is as much to do with ensuring that hosting the Olympics is not a privilege restricted to large, industrially advanced countries, as much as ensuring that the countries that do win the Games budget carefully and do not incur long-term debt. The IOC's response to these very real concerns is however rather one-sided. Its legacy focus is on keeping costs down, rather than on the quality of the spending.

The IOC . . . wants to ensure that the host cities and their residents are left with the most positive legacy of venues, infrastructure, expertise and experience. This can be obtained only through careful definition of the Olympic Games 'standard' requirements and through firm control over the constant inflation of expectations, which has been the trend during recent Olympiads (Olympic Games Study Commission 2003).

While the emphasis on keeping costs down to only necessary spending is to be welcomed, it is not the case that reduced costs will automatically result in greater benefits. If the problem with past Olympics is that there is mismatch between spending on Olympic infrastructure and the long term needs of the host community, just spending less will not close this gap. The negative consequences of adopting too narrow a cost-cutting approach to legacy is illustrated by some of the recommendations that the IOC make, which could actually inhibit other objectives including social and economic sustainability. For example, both the 2002 Commonwealth Games in Manchester and the 2000 Sydney Olympics had volunteer programmes that, at the very least, contributed to a sense of local ownership of the Games. The Olympic Games Study Commission (2003) report however, suggests that volunteers are an area that could be cut back in a bid to reduce the number of accredited people at an Olympics. Equally, the IOC makes some recommendations that could reduce the opportunity for host cities to develop certain supply and service sectors. Instead of favouring local procurement of Olympic facilities, they suggest that the same providers should work across different Olympic Games (Recommendation 3.05, Olympic Games Study Commission 2003).

UK and London Government Policy: accelerating regional development
The London 2012 Bid and the related investment drawn in its wake tessellate with the Government's efforts to promote regeneration in the Thames Gateway. London's population is projected to grow by 810,000 people in the next twelve years, a significant proportion of which is anticipated to be in the region stretching from the East End

of London to the mouth of the Thames Estuary (Mayor of London 2004). The Sustainable Communities Plan (ODPM 2003) outlines the need for 200,000 additional new homes in the Greater South East over the next twenty five years, along with massive new improvements to transport infrastructure. The London Plan (Mayor of London 2004) suggests that by 2016 London will need to accommodate 396,000 additional homes and 636,000 jobs.

All levels of government argue that an Olympic Games provides the opportunity to deliver regeneration benefits to East London, within the context of the broader Sustainable Communities Plan agenda. For example, the then regeneration minister, Tony McNulty MP (2003), has explained that the Government is backing the Bid as it 'is good news for the Thames Gateway and will form part of the long term programme to create new sustainable communities. We will . . . ensure that the emerging detailed proposals for the Olympics will complement this activity and deliver a legacy of thriving, successful, sustainable communities to the east of London.'

Meanwhile, the Mayor of London, Ken Livingstone (2003) has unequivocally argued that:

> The Olympics will bring the biggest single transformation of the city since the Victorian age. It will regenerate East London and bring in jobs and massive improvements in transport infrastructure.

It is hoped that the Olympic Bid will encourage further investment in the Thames Gateway from the private sector and if successful also provide a milestone that infrastructure improvements will have to meet. The Bid process itself has been used as a means to encourage the setting of deadlines, regardless of whether London ultimately gets selected. For example, the Thames Gateway Bridge between Thamesmead and Gallions Reach is now scheduled to be ready by 2012, as will improvements to the Docklands Light Railway and the East London Line. In doing so it is hoped that the Olympic Bid can galvanise local authorities, government and regeneration agencies to create the governance platform to develop the region.

Business: sustaining London's competitive edge

As a city marketing event, the Olympics has a global reach like no other, and business is keen to use this to help London retain its competitive edge. London topped the 2003 annual survey of European cities as the best European city in which to locate a business (Cushman *et al* 2003). London wants to keep it this way and also guard against rising stars in China, India and elsewhere.

Early last year the London Business Board (an overarching body, comprising of the London Chamber of Commerce and Industry, the London CBI and London First) submitted a report to the House of Commons Select Committee outlining why a bid should be made for the Games. They identified three main benefits that could flow from a London 2012 Games. First, benefits from inward investment; an estimated £2 billion was spent by inbound tourism in the wake of the Sydney Games in 2000. Second, a boost for UK exports; again citing Sydney where hosting the Games enabled Australian companies to win ten per cent of capital projects in Beijing, amounting to £1.1 billon of business. Third, a general boost for a wide range of sectors including construction, property, hospitality, leisure and retail, ICT, healthcare, higher and further education, media and the creative industries. Adding to the list of potential business legacies, Martin Crookston identifies in Chapter 2 that the New South Wales government have also claimed the Sydney Games secured £380 million worth of international business conferences.

The Media: transport fixes

After the short listed cities were announced in May, the media in London were quick to emphasise the need for London to improve its transportation system if it is to win the Games. The haphazard planning of the Games in Athens and London's poor showing on transport in the IOC shortlistings in May have added weight to these concerns. The finger is pointed at the tube network, and newspapers, led by the Evening Standard, that rely heavily upon circulation amongst tube users and commuters, have been running an almost campaigning line that the Underground will need to be augmented if London is to win. One such headline read: 'Transport System Rules out Olympics Capital'. What does not get mentioned in the media was the fact the most of the other short listed cities also received a poor rating from the IOC for their public transport support.

Community Dividend: raising local living standards
Several groups in London have been developing an agenda for using the Olympics as a bargaining tool to attain benefits for disadvantaged people living in the East End. For example, the London Citizens Forum, a conglomeration of the East and the South London Communities Organisations, has been championing this agenda. The ideas they are promoting include an Olympic village that provides 60 per cent affordable housing; 30 per cent of construction jobs to go to local builders; and a living wage of £6.70 per hour (£12,194 pa) be paid to all new jobs in the Lower Lea Valley. (This equates to £2.20 higher than the current minimum wage for workers over twenty two years old).

London 2012: a once in a lifetime opportunity . . . for everything
As the overview above clearly shows, the prospect of a London Games has excited a lot of interest and expectations. This is something the Bid Team's approach seems to have actively encouraged as part of its efforts to get people behind the bid. The Games are very much being cast as a 'once in a lifetime' opportunity to regenerate the East End of London:

> All development would form part of an enormous and tangible legacy, ranging from sport and venues through to infrastructure and environment. [The Games] would form part of the most extensive transformation of the city for generations. And its legacy would transform one of the most underdeveloped areas of the country for generations to come . . . thousands of jobs would be created in construction, thousands more as the redevelopment moved ahead and created new businesses and communities (London 2012 2004a).

The cheers would echo down the years. Sport in London and the entire UK would be enhanced forever. The Games would inspire a new generation of athletes and provide wonderful facilities for them. Grassroots participation would be boosted. An already sports-mad nation would get fitter and healthier (London 2012 2004b).

The intensely competitive nature of the bidding process drives this kind of dynamic – London's rivals are mostly capital cities (Madrid, Moscow, Paris and New York) all with a strong global reach. London must raise interest and enthusiasm for the London Bid at both the global and local level, developing messages that resonate with both audiences and also distinguish it from the other bidding cities. However, there are dangers here, London must not make unrealistic promises that cannot be met. Firstly, grand claims may be met with local scepticism – the Lower Lea Valley and surrounding boroughs have seen a number of 'flagship projects' over the years that promise significant regeneration, yet as outlined below, these are areas that continue to experience high levels of disadvantage. Secondly, the evidence from past Games shows a mixed record at best for host cities securing significant positive legacies from staging the Games. It is to these issues that the chapter now turns.

The legacy of past Olympic Games

Rome's 1960 Games marked the point where Olympics began to reach a size where they had a substantial impact on the host city (Chalkley and Essex 1999b). Since then most city leaders have embraced the Olympics as a way of driving through and accelerating change. The Olympics now stands as the largest and boldest form of a model of urban development which really came of age in the late 1980s and early 1990s – city boosterism. A strategy based around marketing, branding and mega-events, it has been embraced by many city leaders as a way for formerly industrial and manufacturing cities to find a new economic base through culture, leisure and tourism.

Hosting major events – and there are none as major as the Olympic Games – is seen as one way to do this, not least because it showcases the city on an international stage.

While nearly all bidding cities have signed up to this broad idea of the Olympics as a driver of urban change, it is less clear exactly what kind of change an Olympics is meant to bring in its wake and there is a serious lack of rigorous research into the benefits and costs associated with holding this, the flagship of the flagship events. For example, there is little detailed research on the employment benefits (Loftman and Spirou 1996), the opportunity costs (Swann 2001) or the social impacts (Spring 2003) of hosting mega-sporting-events. This evidence gap has also been acknowledged by the Government's recent *Game Plan* document (DCMS/Cabinet Office 2002),which admits that it is unclear precisely what types of renewal and regeneration mega-sporting-events contribute to. Within this context of a lack of robust and detailed data and analysis, Box 1.1 is an attempt to bring together what evidence is available about the legacies of recent Summer Olympic and Paralympic Games. There are three headline legacy claims that Olympic Game organisers make:

Physical infrastructure

Although varying in extent between Games all host cities require some new Games related facilities and developments. Land reclamation, improved transport and communications infrastructure, new sporting facilities and housing developments are the most commonly cited legacies. Many host cities report that the Games provide a focus and clear deadline that helps mobilise resources and fast-track development that otherwise would have been slow in its progress or terminally stalled. For example, it has been claimed that the Barcelona Games brought forward fifty years of investment in eight years (Davy and Fickling 2002). A similar argument is being used in London, as reflected in its 'once in a lifetime opportunity for the Lower Lea Valley' campaign line.

Box 1.1: The legacy of recent Olympic Games

Seoul 1988

Motivation/objectives: Prestige; opening economy to outside world.
Infrastructure developments: New sports facilities (inc .Olympic stadium); expansion of Kimpo International Airport; catalyst for new roads, underground stations and telecomms; address environmental and flooding problems in the Chamsil area; Olympic village built as new urban centre with housing, transport, community and retail facilities.
Infrastructure investment (US$bn at 1995 prices): 3.132 (46% public)
Economic impact (estimated net impact/annual city GDP): 1.4%

Barcelona 1992

Motivation/objectives: Urban regeneration catalyst; provide new infrastructure; prestige.
Infrastructure developments: Significant new development embedded into broader 'urban renewal' agenda; new sports facilities (inc. Olympic stadium); new roads, housing and telecomms; Olympic Village built as a new urban centre (housing, transport, community facilities and retail); the harbour area opened up.
Infrastructure investment: 9.105 (38% public)
Economic impact: 2.9%
Games-related employment: Peak of 92,570 (1991), with 20,000 sustained after the Games (12,500 of which are in tourism).

Atlanta 1996

Motivation/objectives: Prestige; economic development; enhance the immediate area surrounding the Olympic Park.
Infrastructure developments: Few new sports facilities (although did include Olympic Stadium which became home to the Atlanta Braves); upgrade Hartsfield International Airport; telecomms network; no new housing (in fact 5,000 public units cleared) as Olympic Village was Georgia Institute of Technology's residences.
Infrastructure investment: 0.990 (15% public)
Economic impact: 0.07%

Sydney 2000

Motivation/objectives: International positioning; promote tourism and convention industries; environmental improvements.

Infrastructure developments: New sports facilities (inc. Olympic Stadium); telecomms; land remediation in Homebush Bay; Olympic Village built as new suburb (Newington) with housing (2,000 dwellings and 5,000 people in the world's largest solar powered settlement, with international benchmarking on waste reduction, water re-use, use of recyclable materials), sports, retail, commercial and transport facilities; catalyst for expansion of Sydney airport including new rail link and road, new parks

Infrastructure investment: Estimated 1.601, although this figure excludes expenditure on the Eastern Distributor road link and the Sydney Airport upgrade (inc. new rail link) (30% public).

Economic impact: 1.0%

Games-related employment: Estimates vary between 90,000-105,000 Games –related jobs.

Athens 2004

Motivation/objectives: Promote tourism and convention industry; reinvent Athens on international stage; environmental improvements.

Infrastructure developments: New sports facilities (inc. Olympic stadium); land remediation, landscaping and remodelling of residential districts, which includes a new urban centre with housing, transport, office space, community and retail facilities, and plans to reduce car use and extend pedestrianisation; new Athens International Airport; ring road; a Metro (by 2010); city precinct revitalisation; create Europe's largest park at Hellenikon; 14,000 new trees planted.

Infrastructure investment: Estimated 4.620 (60% approx public)

Economic impact: Estimated at least 4.1%

Games-related employment: Estimated 150,000

Sources: MacKay and Plumb (2001); Preuss (2000); PricewaterhouseCoppers (2002); OCA (2001); Arthur Andersen (2000); Washington Times (2004); Yu (2004); Daly and Fickling (1997); Rennie Short (2003); Andranovich *et al* (2001); Brunet (1995)

Economic dividend

Most host cities have an explicit aim to leave a beneficial economic legacy – including job creation, new trading opportunities and the enhancement of local, regional and national supply chains. After the Games have finished organisers hope the host city will receive a substantial boost in tourism and convention trade. Indeed, in a desire to showcase the city, the location of Olympic facilities is often a strategic choice. One of the most elegant examples of this was Barcelona's diving pool: located on high ground overlooking the city, TV cameras covering the events could not avoid beaming stunning pictures of the city to viewers all over the world.

Self image and city image

The third common legacy often sited by host cities is that of an altered perception of a city or even a nation – both externally and internally. Externally, the Olympics offers a global platform for cities to project a new image of themselves. For example, Barcelona branded itself as the Catalan capital, Atlanta as a global business city, and Beijing is busy projecting itself as an 'open city'. The targets of these rebranding exercises range from other governments, inward investors and tourists. Internally, the impact within the host city is most often expressed in terms of a 'buzz' that can contribute to increased feelings of patriotism, community spirit and desire to volunteer (Waitt 2003). Perhaps one of the most successful rebranding strategies to date was Sydney's, which projected an image of Australia as a 'can-do nation', successfully playing to both internal and external audiences.

As with other competitions between cities, such as the Capital of Culture, bidding cities are prone to advocacy rather than evidence when making their legacy claims. The result is often a mix of unfulfilled prophecies and unintended consequences, all compounded by the difficulty of isolating what costs and benefits are attributable to the Games and what are the product of wider processes and events. Some of the most common problems that hide behind the PR gloss include:

Community disconnect

Despite sometimes massive infrastructure investment and redevelopment programmes, benefits fail to flow to the people and communities most in need. For example, the widely shared verdict on Atlanta Games is that they left little positive legacy to the city as a whole. Local communities are concerned that many of the benefits promised before the Games were not delivered upon, and the development around the Olympic stadium has only benefited those wealthy enough to live in the new loft apartments (French and Disher 1997). Even Barcelona, which is seen by many as leaving the most positive of Olympic legacies, has suffered some unintended consequences. As Mike Raco argues in Chapter 4, the Olympic Village housing has become increasingly exclusive and triggered a rise in cost of living in the surrounding communities.

White elephants

Without a thoughtful post-Games strategy, spectacular stadiums can have a tendency to turn into a drain on city funds often with overcapacity problems. Even Sydney has been struggling to secure sufficient post-Games use for its Olympic sports facilities (Searle 2002). One recent figure puts the annual shortfall being met through public funding at AUS$46 million a year (*Sydney Morning Herald* 2004). Worse still, Montreal will not finish paying for its Olympic stadium until 2006 – thirty years after it held the Games (Colville 2004).

Sums that do not add up

There is no guaranteed economic dividend from hosting major sporting events. Both Montreal and Munich were left with heavy debts for many years after they hosted the Games (Gratton, Dobson and Shibli 2000).[3] Again, it should be stressed that in terms of the wider economics, the limits of the data and research are apparent and as Martin Crookston argues in Chapter 2, there is little agreement on the economic benefits. However, what is clear is that the estimated net economic impact of the Olympic Games is relatively small in terms of the host city's annual GDP. In absolute terms, the percentages presented in Box 1.1 translate into

US$4–5 billion at 1995 prices in net local economic impact, which would translate into approximately 1.8 per cent of London's current annual GDP.

Vanishing tourists

The record on tourism is mixed. Barcelona, again, is seen as a success story with tourism now a significant sector in the city economy and despite its bad press Atlanta seems to have received a tourism boost (French and Disher 1997). On the other hand, Sydney has seen a twenty five per cent drop in visitor numbers in the two years after the Games. Although this has been blamed on rare events such as September 11 and the SARS virus, the new hotels built for the Olympic Games and in anticipation of a tourism boost, have left a legacy of oversupply and problems within the industry (BBC 2004). And early indications from Athens are of lower than expected tourism figures and ticket sales that are also below expectations (Seager 2004).

Winning a sustainable legacy

So how can London avoid these common Olympic glitches and secure a long-term sustainable legacy? The Games regarded as leaving the most positive legacy is Barcelona. The secret to its success was to tightly weave its Olympics into a much broader and longer strategy of urban renewal, using the Games where appropriate to accelerate development and mobilise resources and investment.

This is an approach that, to an extent, was also adopted by Manchester in running the 2002 Commonwealth Games. According to the Leader of Manchester City Council, Richard Lesse (2003:20), the 'obvious' lesson from Manchester's approach to hosting the Commonwealth Games is that 'regeneration is a holistic exercise that needs planning, and that for an event like the Commonwealth Games to be successful, it had to be just one element of a broader strategy'. Box 1.2 identifies the range of projects that were run alongside the Manchester Commonwealth Games to maximise the opportunity that it presented to 'drive change'. A number of which were

Box 1.2: Programmes run alongside the Manchester Commonwealth Games

The Commonwealth Curriculum Package
This project used the CG to engage school aged children in ICT based learning activities and develop their core ICT skills. Curriculum materials were developed by LEAs across the NW and could be accessed internationally.

Spirit of Friendship Education Programme
Available to all schools to promote understanding of the Commonwealth and global citizenship issues (Commonwealth Curriculum Pack). Schools and pupils were encouraged to organise various Commonwealth-inspired events, such as sports festivals (secondary school pupils organising 'mini' CGs for local primary schools), cultural events and debates and funded through a small grants programme. Launched 2001, 2,000 events held nationwide.

Sportsearch
Part of Sport England's Active Schools initiative, where pupils feed the results of a series of physical tasks into a web-linked PC that identifies the sport their aptitudes suggest they may be best suited to and identifies local facilities they could access.

Passport 2002
A school activity programme through which 13,500 11–18 year olds throughout the North West participated in sporting, cultural and volunteering activities.

Pre-Volunteer Programme
The first of its type. The PVP aimed to ensure that the Games volunteers were drawn from groups who would not normally participate in such activities to improve their skills, confidence and the chance they would go on volunteering. It ran from 1999–2003 and was SRB funded. 6,250 participated, it provided 8% of the main Volunteer programme, and 160 people had secured employment by December 2002.

Volunteer Programme
The main Games volunteer programme recruited over 10,000 people, of which 24 per cent had not previously undertaken any volunteering.

Post-Games Volunteer Programme
A programme that allows both Games and non-Games volunteers to volunteer subsequent events. 2,000 volunteers registered for future events. As of August 2004, ninety events have been supported since the CG.

Queen's Relay
A relay with the baton transported across England, 'showcasing' sports development initiatives, particularly involving young people where possible.

Let's Celebrate
£500,000 provided through the SRB programme to develop the processional and celebratory arts of the North West's South Asian, African and African Caribbean communities. The communities are involved in the process and it is hoped that the events will endure beyond the Games. Funding available from April 2001.

NW Healthier Communities Programme
A programme to build the capacity of community health initiatives across the North West by provide training and support to health projects in the most deprived communities.

Prosperity North West SRB Projects
A programme utilising the Games as a promotional asset for trade and investment.

Games Exchange
A single access point for enquiries and information relating to the Games and the wider opportunities it offered, such as tourism.

Free event tickets
Approximately 550 tickets were secured for the Games as a whole; 1,000 tickets for the Opening Ceremony Test Event; 2,000 for the CG Athletics Trials; and two VIP boxes for the trials and the athletics events. These were secured variously through company donation, the NDC and SAZ and distributed through community groups, residents, schools and sports clubs.

Party in the Parks
Four held (on the two Saturdays and Sundays during the Games), with lots of sporting activities. Each had over 1,000 attendees and the largest had 5,000.

Sources: Faber Maunsell (2004); Sport England

funded through the North West Economic and Social Single Regeneration Budget programme that ran from 1995 to 2001. A Commonwealth Games Opportunities and Legacy Partnership Board was also established in 1999 with three aims: to provide economic, tourism and social benefits across the whole region; to meet the needs of disadvantaged communities in East Manchester through the regeneration programme; and, to provide new opportunities for North West business (Faber Maunsell 2004).[4]

There seem to be two lessons that stand out from the experience of past Games. First, the Olympics must be embedded within a broader strategy of urban renewal and regeneration if they are to lever maximum benefit. On their own, Olympics do not deliver significant, sustainable benefits. If an Olympic Games is to contribute towards a sustainable legacy, it must provide more than new facilities; it must be part of an urban regeneration programme that has both social and economic aims.

Second, given this, a significant proportion of the legacy from a London 2012 Games will be delivered before any Games are held. For maximum benefit the Olympics must be integrated into existing, or stimulate the creation of new, programmes from the outset. As this chapter will now go on to identify, the scale of the regeneration challenge for a London Games is large.

The scale of the challenge

In some aspects the impact of a 2012 London Games will be felt most significantly in surrounding areas of the main site – the Lower Lea Valley (LLV). This is an area with a significant industrial and post-industrial landscape, forming part of four east London boroughs – Hackney, Newham, Tower Hamlets and Waltham Forest – with the Millennium Dome in Greenwich also being used as a venue. As discussed above, London 2012 and the other stakeholders are presenting the Games as a 'once in a lifetime opportunity' to regenerate the LLV and the surrounding area (hereafter referred to as the Olympic boroughs). The LLV has been identified as an 'Opportunity Area' in the Mayor of London's

Table 1.1: The population of the Lower Lea Valley

	Total (000's)	Population Change 1982-2002 %	Mean age[1]	UK	Rep of Ireland	Other EU[2]	Non-EU
					Country of Birth (%)[1]		
Hackney	210	14.9	32.92	65.53	2.09	2.89	29.48
Newham	254	20.1	31.75	61.82	0.97	1.60	35.61
Tower Hamlets	207	44.1	31.85	64.96	1.37	2.51	30.85
Waltham Forest	223	3.6	35.13	74.76	1.63	1.89	21.72
Greenwich	221	3.3	35.67	81.96	1.59	1.76	14.70
5 Olympic boroughs (ave)	223	17.2	33.46	69.80	1.53	2.13	26.47
London	7,355	8.7	36.33	75.16	2.06	2.92	19.85
England	49,559	5.9	38.65	91.08	0.91	1.38	6.63
UK	59,229	5.2	38.60	91.65	0.91	1.32	6.12

Sources: ONS (2004a; 2004b)
Notes: 1 The England figure here refers to England and Wales
2 EU defined on Census Day (19 April 2001)

Table 1.2: Level of highest qualification held by people of working age by Local Education Authority, 2002/03 (%)

	Level 4 and above	Level 3	Below Level 2	Level 2	No Qualifications
Hackney	31.6	13.5	14.7	19.3	20.8
Newham	16.1	14.4	19.3	22.6	27.7
Tower Hamlets	26.3	13.7	16.3	16.8	26.9
Waltham Forest	24.5	13.1	19.8	21.9	20.7
Greenwich	26.0	17.3	22.7	19.2	14.8
5 Olympic boroughs (ave)	24.9	14.4	18.56	19.96	22.18
London	30.5	15.9	20.1	19.6	13.9
England	23.9	18.7	21.9	20.1	15.4

Source: ONS (2004c)
Notes: Level 4+ = higher education;
Level 3 = 2 or more A levels or advanced vocational qualification;
Level 2 = 5 or more higher grade GCSEs or intermediate vocational qualification;
Level 1 and other = lower grade GCSEs or lower level vocational or foreign qualifications.

Table 1.3: Claimants of key benefits[1] in London boroughs, November 03
(% of working age population by statistical group and local authority)

	All	Unemployed	Sick and Disabled	Lone Parents	Other
Hackney	23.3	5.6	10.5	5.9	1.3
Newham	19.4	4.3	9.3	5.0	0.7
Tower Hamlets	20.8	5.9	9.5	4.5	0.9
Waltham Forest	15.5	3.9	7.2	3.6	0.8
Greenwich	18.2	5.9	12.3	6.9	1.0
5 Olympic Boroughs (ave)	19.44	5.12	9.76	5.18	0.94
London[2]	14.2	3.3	7	3.2	0.6
Great Britain Total (including Overseas)	13.9	2.5	8.7	2.2	0.5

Sources: ONS (2004d; 2004e)

Notes: 1 Key benefits are Jobseeker's Allowance (JSA), Incapacity Benefit (IB), Severe Disablement Allowance, Disability Living Allowance.
2 This figure is for February 2004.

(2004) London Plan, with significant new development to help accommodate London's growing population. The institutional focus and extra resources associated with a London 2012 Games may well present an opportunity to jump start this development.

The Olympic boroughs are an area with significant assets. They are close to central London; have a significant transport hub at Stratford; have extensive waterways; have a rich industrial archaeology and heritage which provides an enduring visual and physical legacy; a vibrant multi-cultural history; and have a rich cultural and sporting heritage. As Tables 1.1 and 1.2 demonstrate, the Olympic boroughs are also an area where the population has been growing in recent years, helping to create a relatively young, mixed community with a high graduate population in national terms (although, with the exception of Greenwich they also suffer from a very high proportion of working age residents with no qualifications).

Any new development must, therefore, be careful to build upon and enhance these existing assets. The Olympic boroughs are also, however, areas of significant disadvantage. If the new developments are to be used as a tool for regeneration, particularly in the LLV, it is important to gain a clear understanding of the nature of the problems facing the area. Any programmes and policies designed to deliver local benefits must take account of the significant disadvantage experienced by many within the Olympic boroughs.

Along the Government's Index of Multiple Deprivation (IMD), the five Olympic boroughs are some of the most deprived areas in the UK. Scratching beneath this aggregate figure we can identify some of the key indicators of this disadvantage. Table 1.3 shows that all of the Olympic boroughs suffer high levels of unemployment. Hackney, Tower Hamlets and Greenwich are particularly disadvantaged with unemployment figures over twice the average for Great Britain, with Newham and Waltham Forest only faring a little better. Moreover, unemployment figures do not capture the true extent of inactivity, with the numbers of people claiming sickness and disability benefits often double the unemployment figure. Table 1.3 graphically demonstrates the level of inactivity in all the Olympic boroughs is significantly above the average for Great Britain and London as a whole.

It is important to note that this concentration of significant economic inactivity in the Olympic boroughs occurs despite the fact they are part of the UK's most prosperous region. According to Buck et al (2002:199) while inner East London has had 'a history of underemployment stretching back in the nineteenth century . . . the current pattern of very highly concentrated unemployment in this area only seems to have emerged during the last twenty years, against a background of relatively strong performance in the regional economy'. The authors go on to argue that there are complex socio-economic processes producing this geography of disadvantage, with 'selective patterns of population decentralisation' (Buck et al 2002:36) leaving inner east London boroughs with residual populations suffering from multiple disadvantage.

This pattern seems to hold true for other policy areas. For example, whilst Table 1.4 paints a positive picture in terms of the levels of youth unemployment in the Olympic boroughs, it does show starkly

Table 1.4: Percentage of unemployed by classification by London borough, 2001

	Aged 16–24	Who have never worked	Who are long-term unemployed[2]
Hackney	19.39	16.93	32.81
Tower Hamlets	24.65	13.99	33.05
Newham	25.16	20.99	30.93
Waltham Forest	23.57	13.42	33.02
Greenwich	23.61	13.71	34.61
5 Olympic Boroughs (ave)	23.28	15.80	32.88
London[1]	21.50	12.18	30.70
England and Wales	25.90	9.26	30.32

Source: ONS (2004f)

Notes: 1 The Greater London Urban Area
          2 Those who stated they had not worked since 1999 or earlier.

that the Olympic boroughs all have above average levels of long-term unemployed and have disturbingly high levels of unemployed residents who have never worked.

The Olympic boroughs also suffer from educational underachievement. As Table 1.5 demonstrates, at both Key Stage 2 and 3, all four Local Education Authorities (LEAs) perform below the average for

Table 1.5: Pupil performance at Key Stage 2 and 3 by LEA, 2003

	% achieving Level 4+ at KS2[1]			% achieving Level 5+ KS3[2]		
	English	Maths	Science	English	Maths	Science
Hackney	63	59.2	75	59	52	47
Newham	68.5	66.5	80.5	55	60	53
Tower Hamlets	74	71.4	83.3	55	55	46
Waltham Forest	69.7	68.4	80.6	60	62	59
Greenwich	69.9	66.5	81.7	61	61	54
5 Olympic Boroughs (ave)	69.02	66.4	79.62	58	58	51.8
England	75	73	87	69	71	68

Sources: DfES (2003a; 2003b)

Notes: 1 Level 4 is the level expected of most 11 year olds.
           2 Level 5 or 6 is the level of achievement expected of most pupils at the end of KS3.

Table 1.6: Working age employment by qualification level by LEA, 2002/03 (%)

	Overall	Level 4 and above	Level 3	Below Level 2	Level 2	No Qualifications
Hackney	60.0	84.4	57.7	53.6	49.1	38.8
Newham	52.7	80.7	60.3	53.7	54.7	30.1
Tower Hamlets	52.5	88.7	49.2	44.1	46.9	27.4
Waltham Forest	68.7	88.6	80.1	69.1	61.1	45.6
Greenwich	64.8	88.1	69.2	67.5	49.9	33.9
5 Olympic boroughs (ave)	59.74	86.1	63.3	57.6	52.34	35.16
England	74.5	86.3	78.4	76.3	73.4	50.6

Source: ONS (2004c)

England in terms of achieving the expected levels of attainment. Hackney, Newham and Tower Hamlets can again be seen to be particularly bad performers. Also striking is the decline in performance between Key Stages 2 and 3. Although consistently below the English average at Key Stage 2, this English average to LEA gap in attainment at Key Stage 3 is significantly worse for all four authorities.

This low education achievement is obviously a problem in itself. But as Table 1.6 demonstrates, it seems to have a significant influence on an individual's employment rate. Across all boroughs there is a significant variation in employment rate by qualification level. Although there is quite wide variation between the boroughs, when their individual rates are compared to the national figures the overall working age employment rate is significantly lower. At Level 4+ the boroughs do have strong employment rates. However, the employment rate drops significantly at lower qualification levels, and those with qualifications below Level 2 have particularly low employment rates.

In health the data is harder to access. In terms of 'hard' data, the Standard Mortality Ratio (SMR) for the Olympic boroughs is above the UK average, especially in Newham and Tower Hamlets (Table 1.7). Further, a recent Greater London Authority/London Health Commission report, *Health in London*, cited results from the 2001

Table 1.7: Health and illness in selected London boroughs

	SMR[2] (UK=100)	Limiting long-term illness (%)		Self-assessed general health (%)		
		Overall	Working age population	Good	Fairly good	Not good
Hackney	101	18.07	15.96	68.36	20.99	10.65
Tower Hamlets	115	17.19	15.02	67.89	21.79	10.32
Newham	119	17.32	15.58	67.95	21.90	10.14
Waltham Forest	110	16.54	13.04	68.60	22.44	8.97
Greenwich	106	17.25	13.69	68.48	22.24	9.28
5 Olympic Boroughs (ave)	110.2	17.27	14,65	68.2	21.87	9.87
London[1]	98	15.31	11.56	71.12	20.84	8.04
England and Wales	98	18.23	13.56	68.55	22.23	9.22

Sources: ONS (2004a; 2004f)

Notes: 1 The Greater London Urban Area
2 The Standard Mortality Ratio takes account of the age structure of the population. The SMR refers to 2001. They are based on the UK population estimates published in September 2003.

Census that identified Hackney, Newham, Waltham Forest and Tower Hamlets as having below average self-reported good health. It also categorised Hackney, Newham and Waltham Forest's infant mortality rates for 1996–2001 as 'significantly high' and indicated that Tower Hamlets' figure was also above average for England and Wales (GLA and London Health Commission 2003).

As the data presented above demonstrates, the Olympic boroughs suffer significant levels of disadvantage. If a London 2012 Games is to meet the UK government's, the Mayor of London's and London 2012's expressed ambition of contributing towards regeneration in the Lower Lea Valley, then the overall approach and specific programmes must address the causes of multiple deprivation in the area. This is especially apparent in the high levels of employment inactivity and the concentration of many people with low skills (and their low employment rate). These data aptly demonstrate the scale of the challenge if new employment opportunities associated with an Olympics are to be accessed by local residents.

The forthcoming chapters

The five chapters all argue that an Olympics will not necessarily deliver a sustainable legacy on its own. Rather, an Olympics must be part of a broader policy agenda and set of programmes that contribute towards regeneration and social policy goals. As Mike Raco argues in Chapter 2, flagship projects such as the Olympics always promise change, but have not always delivered the type of change that is claimed for the Lower Lea Valley. For this to be avoided, Mike argues that there must be significant 'bottom-up' involvement in the Olympic process. Moreover, the Olympics must be embedded with existing projects, agencies and partnerships.

Martin Crookston (Chapter 3) makes a similar argument in the employment legacy chapter. Although Martin cautions against some of the inflated claims surrounding the benefits that major events can deliver, he does argue that through appropriate planning a London 2012 Games could deliver employment benefits to deprived communities. However, this will require a significant amount of work, with a need to change current practice in some areas. Without training programmes for the unemployed, different hiring practices from companies and a different approach from the authorities in how they deal with both groups, any employment opportunities may pass deprived individuals by.

The need to adopt new practices is also a central theme in Roger Levett's environmental legacy chapter (Chapter 4). Roger argues that a positive green legacy is possible for a London Olympics, but to achieve this will require more than simply minimising the environmental impact of a Games. It will require new practices and new behaviours being adopted and the Olympics to serve as a model of best practice that could be adopted more widely. But to achieve this, strong environmental principles must be embedded into a London Olympics' planning, management and decision making processes.

Fred Coalter makes a similar argument for the sports legacy in Chapter 5. Fred argues that if an Olympics is to deliver a sustainable sporting legacy, it must contribute towards the Government's *Game Plan* target of increasing sports participation. After providing a detailed account of past Games' record in increasing sports participation, Fred argues that the focus must be on grassroots sport, with proactive policies that embed the Olympics within existing and new policies and programmes.

The final legacy theme chapter is Keith Khan's cultural legacy chapter (Chapter 6). Keith argues for a London 2012 Olympic Cultural Programme to leave a positive legacy, it must contribute towards an improved understanding of both the self and the other. Resonating with the other chapters, Keith argues that an Olympic Cultural Programme should therefore be embedded within a broader cultural project that explores, and even reassesses, London and the UK and their place within the world.

All of these chapters contain a host of ideas that aim to help make London's bid distinctive and innovative and also help set the foundations for sustainable legacy. They all argue that a London 2012 Games does provide an opportunity to deliver lasting benefits, but early planning and an embedding within existing policy agendas and programmes will be essential. The conclusion (Chapter 7) picks up a number of these themes and outlines in more detail what this means for a London 2012 Games. It also identifies nine practical policy ideas that could help secure a sustainable Olympic legacy.

2 Whose Gold Rush? The social legacy of a London Olympics

Mike Raco

2 Whose Gold Rush?

The social legacy of a London Olympics

Mike Raco

> The Olympic Games and Paralympic Games can rightly claim to be the greatest show on earth . . . They leave a host of indelible memories but also long-lasting benefits for the cities and countries that host them (Tony Blair 2004).

There is little doubt that the coming of an Olympic Games to London in 2012 would have a major impact on the social, political and economic fortunes of the city and the rest of the UK. The Olympic Games is seen as a prize that will transform the image of London and bring about significant improvements in its infrastructure and levels of tourism and inward investment. Since the late 1970s flagship events, such as Olympic Games, have become a core feature of urban, regional and national development strategies across the world. They can generate opportunities for radical and significant regeneration by bringing new jobs, investment, and hope back to areas that have suffered from severe and on-going de-industrialisation. As Essex and Chalkley (1998:202) note: 'the scale of investment required for the Games has become so great that it might be argued that the concept of sport as a means of spiritual renewal has given way to sport as a means of urban renewal'. In a context of enhanced global capital mobility, territorial competition and cross-border investment, such events provide a 'focus' for the creation of new development agendas (Cheshire and Gordon 1998).

However, the beneficial impacts of flagship projects are not as straightforward as is often claimed. In many cases, they enhance socio-economic inequalities between communities by increasing costs of living and doing little to increase employment opportunities or material incomes for the most deprived (Hall and Hubbard 1998).

They can create islands of development that barely connect to the localities in which they are situated. This chapter examines the evidence from flagship and sport-led regeneration programmes over recent decades and assesses the possible impacts of an Olympic Games on residential and business communities in the East End of London. It raises some key themes from earlier studies concerning the social impacts of such events and assesses how the benefits from a Games can be shared by a wider range of interests and communities. The chapter begins by examining the effects of top down strategies before turning to a discussion of New Labour's community-focused programmes and what issues need to be addressed if a London Games is to deliver an inclusive and socially-sustainable set of legacies. Collectively, the chapter argues that an Olympic Games will not be able to solve the social and economic problems of East London alone and that it will need to be embedded into a wider range of projects if it is to deliver a progressive social legacy. It if does so it could provide an opportunity to kick start development in one of Britain's most disadvantaged urban areas, secure wider social dividends and act as an example of regeneration best practice that could also benefit the UK as a whole.

Flagship events and social legacies – change, continuity and community

A large body of research has examined the strengths, weaknesses and broader social impacts of flagship projects and three inter-related themes can be identified from the literature:

Prioritising change over continuity

Flagship projects are often associated with grandiose claims of economic growth, urban regeneration and community riches. They promise radical agendas of socio-economic *change* through which projects will transform 'problem places' into 'opportunity spaces'. Major events such as Olympic Games or World Cups tend to be promoted as 'once in a lifetime' opportunities for development, with the corollary that a failure to attract them represents a 'once in a lifetime' *missed* opportunity. Although, clearly, change is an essential ingredient in successful development programmes, there is a danger that existing forms of employment and local attachments to the social or cultural value of places earmarked for regeneration may be overlooked and undervalued. For example, many 'deprived' urban areas possess successful manufacturing firms that employ local people and thrive as a consequence of low rents and lack of developer interest (Imrie and Thomas 1995). Their clearance, in the name of change, can have damaging social impacts on local communities as occurred in Barcelona in 1992 where hundreds of thriving small businesses were evicted from the Olympic area (Shapcott 1998). At the same time other sites that appear to be vacant or derelict to outsiders may in fact possess significant heritage or environmental value (English Heritage 2004). The failure to build on the *existing strengths and continuities* of regeneration areas has resulted in many flagship projects and spectacle-based forms of development failing to engage with local communities' needs and aspirations. Indeed, often implicit in such programmes is the need to change 'problem' communities entirely through processes of gentrification and displacement.

Community ownership, decision-making processes and the governance of flagship developments

A key element in the success of any event is the extent to which it generates *ownership* in local communities over the direction and outcomes of project spending and how regeneration aims and objectives are established and prioritised. One of biggest criticisms of flagship programmes is that they are shaped by powerful, non-local agents whose main concern is to maximise profit returns at the expense of the social and economic needs of local communities. As Jones (2001:53) argues in a context of 'growth spurred by media coverage and visitation, and expenditure impacts, the attraction of overseas and business spectators becomes of paramount importance and local acceptance and participation of lesser importance'. The consequences of this are two fold. First, the focus becomes one of 'getting the event', whatever the cost. Development agendas are set by external agencies and as Cochrane *et al*'s (2003:106–7) study of Manchester's Olympic bid shows cities 'pledge higher and higher levels of local financial support, servicing and infrastructure provision, and trade concessions with the IOC (for example concerning TV rights [and] merchandising) . . . simply in order to stay in the Olympic competition'. This is often at the expense of strategic thinking about how such events are to be embedded into a wider set of development agendas that, for instance, promote community-based training or encourage investment in wider social projects such as health and education initiatives. Second, community priorities may be pushed to one side as bidders strive to present a united front, built around well organised development partnerships dominated by 'movers and shakers'. This generates conformity and limits the extent of 'bottom-up' participation in setting development priorities. The legitimacy of community criticism is often undermined and branded as 'irresponsible', or in the case of the Sydney Games, 'unpatriotic' (Hillier 1988; Waitt 1999).

Promoting development in rather than development of host cities
Flagship events generate significant economic activity and there has been growing interest in how they can contribute to neighbourhood renewal.[1] New facilities and employment opportunities are often perceived *a priori* to be of benefit to local communities. However, the trickle-down effects of flagship projects are notoriously erratic. For example, jobs in the construction sector are often tied to multinational companies whose labour is only partially drawn from surrounding areas (Turok 1992). Even in economic terms, the track record of sporting projects is far from clear. For example, Chaplin's (2004) study of the impacts of sporting stadia and events on economic development in thirty four North America cities indicates that although US$18 billion was invested in new stadiums alone during the 1990s, the direct impacts on neighbourhoods were difficult to establish. Noll and Zimblast's (1997:2) assessment of such developments similarly concludes that 'a new sports facility has an extremely small (perhaps even negative) effect on overall economic activity

and employment'. Meanwhile, the indirect impacts of processes of gentrification and price inflation can be severe. In Barcelona, for instance, the 1992 Games was partly responsible for massive increases in costs of living in the city. Between 1986 and 1992 the market price of housing grew by an average of 260 per cent and this expansion continued through the 1990s with significant increases in social inequality (Hughes 2001). Likewise, in Sydney rates of evictions and homelessness increased markedly in the neighbourhoods alongside the Olympic development (Martinez 2001). The consequence is that although development takes place in such cities it does not always lead to the development of its poorer urban neighbourhoods and communities. In fact, it can make things worse by creating blight, congestion and community displacement.

Sustainable regeneration and embedded development – building Olympic legacies from the bottom up

Given the track record of flagship projects outlined above, how can an event like an Olympic Games be used to promote locally-sensitive and socially sustainable regeneration? Is it always the case that such events generate new forms of inequality or can measures be put in place to ensure that local communities and businesses gain lasting benefits in social and economic terms? The neighbourhoods alongside the London Olympic Park site are amongst the most deprived in the UK and suffer from acute problems of poor housing, low levels of employment and skills, low educational attainment, high mortality rates and poor environmental quality.[2] If the Olympic Games is to be judged as 'successful' then the quality of life in such neighbourhoods needs to be significantly improved. In short, it needs to generate development of, not just development in, local areas. This section examines how such processes might occur and what policy issues need to be addressed from the bidding stage of the process onwards. It argues that a Games could represent a pivotal moment in re-shaping the (geographical) investment priorities of governments and the private sector and change the perceptions of the East End. However, it begins by examining how the Games relates to New Labour's broader regeneration programmes and what lessons can be gained from their experiences.

New Labour, community-led regeneration and the Olympic bid

The emergence of a London Olympic Games Bid is, in many ways, out of character with the broader thrust of New Labour's regeneration policies since 1997 (for a review see Imrie and Raco 2003). Flagship policies have been out of fashion as the Government has divorced itself from the socially-divisive programmes that characterised urban policy in the 1980s and early 1990s (Cochrane 2003). The focus has, instead, been on area-based programmes with communities playing a role as both policy objects – those who are to be worked on and assisted – and policy subjects – those who actively develop and implement policy measures. A range of initiatives, from the New Deal for Communities (NDC) programme to the Neighbourhood Renewal Fund have drawn on the principles of local partnership working and community inclusion, albeit within a context of centrally-defined government objectives and targets. Active citizenship has become the buzzword with communities and individuals expected (and sometimes compelled) to take increased responsibility for themselves and their neighbourhoods.

The experiences of these programmes to date have clear lessons for an Olympic Games programme as well as new development and regeneration programmes more broadly. For example, one recurring theme has been that of community capacities and the ability of communities and individuals to engage in bureaucratic and technocratic structures of policy making and delivery. To qualify for government spending, projects have to satisfy strict auditing procedures. For some organisations, such as local authorities, this presents few barriers to effective working. However, for poorly-funded and under-trained community representatives, such mechanisms stretch their capacities to be active participants and limit the scope and forcefulness of community consultation. Likewise, other stakeholders, such as business representatives or public sector agencies, can find themselves over-committed to local partnership working and there is clear evidence of 'consultation fatigue' in many areas. So, whilst community activation and local partnership working appear to empower local actors, practical constraints have had a significant impact on the form and character of community involvement – a clear issue facing any 'inclusive' agenda for a London 2012 Olympic Games that will have to set aside resources to underpin community participation.[3]

A related issue is that of community influence in shaping planning agendas. In a number of NDC projects community-led proposals have been rejected by central government on the grounds that they run counter to government policy.[4] By 2002 NDC projects had failed to spend two-thirds of their allocated £360 million as local partnerships because they were unable to jump over the bureaucratic hurdles set by central government when drawing up local strategies (Weaver 2002). As discussed earlier, this can be a significant issue in relation to flagship projects, such as Olympic Games, where the primary responsibility for setting agendas lies with bodies and interests external to the neighbourhoods in which the events take place. What if local residential and business communities actively challenge or oppose the policy trajectories of an Olympic Games? Will mechanisms be established to encourage and embrace such opposition or will local criticism be airbrushed out of the political process on the grounds of being 'irresponsible', 'unrealistic' and contrary to the 'spirit of partnership' surrounding the Games? Such questions have been critical in programmes such as the NDC where a failure by central government to accept the legitimacy of alternative visions has undermined efforts to create a sense of community ownership and commitment.

New Labour's regeneration policies have also run up against difficulties in sustaining community involvement. There tends to be a 'lifecycle' of engagement with participation rising at first and then falling away. Communities are particularly active when addressing short term issues such as the closure of a local hospital or a controversial new housing development (Delanty 2004). It is much more difficult to sustain interest and the commitment of community groups over a longer period of time. In the case of the London 2012 Olympic Games, with its seven-year development cycle, sustaining community interest is going to be a significant challenge.[5] The most successful examples of community engagement are where local partnerships are able to claim visible policy successes and direct benefits from participation and where agencies actively support community participation and mobilisation without placing too many restrictions on it. The next section now examines some of the ways in which lessons from regeneration practices might be taken forwards to establish a more socially-oriented set of development agendas in and around a London 2012 Olympic Games.

Embedding the Games – delivering a socially-oriented development agenda

Whatever the expectations, an Olympic Games on its own will not be able to bring about the wholesale regeneration of the East End of London. While some critics argued that the main development sites, such as Stratford, are already undergoing significant redevelopment and the Olympics may blight existing plans (Rawnsley 2003), the challenge is to ensure that the development associated with a 2012 Games does act as a 'catalyst' for broader development in the Lower Lea Valley. The first step in promoting a Games, therefore, has to be honest public acceptance of its limitations and the promotion of realistic expectations. Rather than seeking to create a limiting 'consensus' about how beneficial a Games would be, the process should be actively politicised so that a range of perspectives, costs and benefits are aired and debated. As with other Olympic Games public 'opinion' has been measured thus far through opinion polls that indicate a high degree of support.[6] In the bidding documents descent is boiled down to one line: 'there is no organised public opposition to hosting the Games in London' (London 2012 2004:12). This positive gloss reflects the broader need for the bid to be seen as popular by the IOC, the media and other external bodies. However, other surveys, that provide respondents with the financial costs of the Games, indicate a much lower level of satisfaction. Only forty four per cent of

Londoners in such a poll supported the project (*The Economist* 2004). Similar criticisms have been made by a range of community and voluntary groups both within the UK (NCVO 2004) and in other cities where Games have taken place, such as Athens (Smith 2004). These need to be reflected in debates over the trajectories of development that result from a Games if it is to deliver socially-oriented forms of development.

Since the 1960s Olympic Games have been used to create new public spaces. In the London bid a thirty five-hectare site in Stratford will house the Olympic Village on which 5,000 new homes will be built under a public-private agreement that 'would have a guaranteed legacy use as affordable housing for key occupations such as teachers and medical personnel' (London 2012 2004:12). In this sense the Games could provide a valuable catalyst for much-needed new housing. However, this proposal will need to be carefully planned and tightly regulated if it is to have wider community benefits. Developers will be keen to use the 'Olympic Village' tag to inflate market values and maximise returns. Inevitable tensions between the social and economic dimensions of this housing will emerge over who, for example, constitutes a 'key worker', how much disposable income such workers have, what price an 'affordable' house should be and what proportion, if any, should be available to those from local communities unable to buy their own property. In Barcelona, the Olympic Village development has been a commercial success story but it has also become increasingly exclusive and has helped to push up the costs of living in adjoining poorer communities, with significant social implications (Hughes 2001). In contrast the Munich Olympic Village site has since become a showcase of regeneration with a strong emphasis on community use and recreation (Synadinos 2001). The track record of creating socially-oriented and inclusive development in Britain is not as positive as the Munich example, with a strong tendency to favour the interests of property developers and their shareholders.

The London Olympic Games could, therefore, set a new example of regeneration best practice by shifting the balance of responsibilities and benefits firmly towards social needs. It could act as a role model for the mobilisation of community activism and local knowledge and act as a significant check on the growing trend towards commercialisation and profiteering. In implementing such agendas, however, there will need to be a clear definition of roles and responsibilities between the various stakeholders involved in the Olympic Games programme. In order to be effective, the Organising Committee will need to tie its community programmes closely to those of existing agencies and partnerships. The Olympic Park site is, for example, a key area within the wider Thames Gateway regeneration and a range of institutions will have responsibilities for different aspects of the development.[7] There is a real possibility of institutional overkill in the proposals and the extent to which these agencies can become 'joined up' in their approach will be critical to the form and character of the developments that take place. Consequently, existing plans, such as Community Strategies and local authority partnerships, will need to be utilised rather than ignored. In addition, a clear set of roles and responsibilities needs to be created for formal community involvement. All the evidence demonstrates that local representation and some devolution of power are vital elements in shaping the trajectories and legacies of development that take place. Again, existing networks could be used to identify key players to perform such a role, even with the inevitable limitations, in terms of capacities and representativeness, that such individuals/organisations bring with them.

There also needs to be active planning over the sustainability and continuity of the regeneration efforts with a trade-off between the needs of a Games in July and August 2012 and longer-term visions for the area. Flagship regeneration programmes are notorious for their failures in identifying clear parameters and objectives beyond the short term. Strategies need to be developed that recognise the significance of what happens when the Games stops acting as a focus for regeneration plans. There is a clear danger of institutional and policy drift, as has been the case with smaller flagship projects such as the Garden Festivals of the 1980s or some of the Millennium projects of the 1990s. In a more practical sense sporting events also leave behind a complex array of physical infrastructure and a range of legacies over issues of ownership and funding. It seems likely, for instance, that the Athens Games will overshoot its original budget of US$5.6 billion creating a deficit that some have claimed may take the country's treasury over ten years to re-pay with other knock-on effects for social and community projects (Smith 2004). Communities and local authorities are often unwilling to pick up the direct costs of maintaining and servicing infrastructure after a Games event is completed, particularly as there are other pressing demands on limited resources. The importance of securing a viable, sustainable role or purpose for a new stadium and other sporting infrastructure following a London Games cannot be overstated. Along the Athens model there is a real danger of them diverting money from other budgets, something that would have a detrimental impact on local communities and voluntary organisations (such as sporting bodies) that rely on low level, small scale grants and projects.

Developing a clear set of timetables and legacy strategies will, therefore, be a central element in ensuring that the longer term impacts of a Games on local services are well planned and co-ordinated. This, in turn, will help to make the event more legitimate to local communities by offering them clear longer term visions of its effects. These liability costs need to shared out between different levels of government and private sector investors and the Games organisers should to be clear about how they will sustain activity around the new sites over subsequent years. The prospect of visibly decaying, under-used and expensive facilities in an area such as the East End would further undermine its image and reputation in the longer term, as well as providing a graphic symbol of how state-backed regeneration programmes channel resources into flagship, short term spectacle projects at the expense of investments in housing and other social infrastructure. The Millennium Dome provides a salient example of this process in action.

The role of funding regimes is also critical. Funds for a Games will be raised through a combination of a one off surcharge of £20 on London Council Tax payers, a new National Lottery Game,[8] government grants and private sector investment. Even with this mix of sources it is estimated that the Games will cost the average London household £279 (*The Economist* 2004) and will require significant corporate backing. This reliance on corporate investors means that ostensibly cities are in a relatively poor bargaining position *vis-à-vis* sporting bodies as the onus is on them to make themselves attractive investment destinations (see Lee 2002). However, with the Olympic Games is this really the case? In a context where companies are increasingly keen to be seen to be 'socially responsible' a high profile Olympic Games provides an opportunity for an Organising Committee to develop a set of reciprocal agreements with sponsors and other investors. These could ensure that there is direct investment in local infrastructure, skills and other people-focused projects, such as child care for working mothers or care for the elderly or disabled. At the same time organisers could also insist that, in return for sponsorship deals, corporate funds could be made available to local community organisations, possibly those created by NDC partnerships, and that a proportion of the tickets for the Games went to local people for a nominal charge.[9] Such moves would provide an opportunity to directly include local people in the events taking place around them in a more meaningful and significant way than some corporate-driven flagship projects (see Jones 2001). Event organisers must not be trapped in 'dependent' relationships in which they concede to the wishes of corporate investors and developers. Instead, they should realise the relative strength of their position and use a Games as a way of publicising good practice in partnership-building by extracting concessions from investors who will not want to miss out on the global coverage and opportunities that such events generate.

Critically, for an Olympic Games to play a significant social role it must be embedded within a broader range of mainstream initiatives and not act as a substitute or alibi for them. For example, a Games is put forward as an opportunity to foster a renaissance in grassroots British sport that will generate a 'boom in our schools and local communities'. (London 2012 2004:2) It will not only improve sporting standards but also promote healthy lifestyles that will benefit participants for the rest of their lives. However, such proclamations are made at the same time as other government agencies and cash-strapped local authorities are significantly reducing the number of school playing fields across the country. In addition, the UK has longer working hours than any other EU country. This reduces opportunities for people to engage in sporting activities, yet the Government shows no signs of agreeing to EU limits. Moreover, a recent report by the Healthcare Commission (2004) highlights the inequalities in health care provision and mortality rates across the UK. A person living in Tower Hamlets, for example, is far more likely to die from heart disease or cancer than a person living in a more affluent part of the country.

The consequences of a Games in terms of health and sporting benefits, therefore needs to be thought through. There is only so much an event can do to tackle structural inequalities in health care, although if the Government is serious about the promotion of sporting activities and improving health levels in deprived areas it needs to think more holistically about the effects of a broad range of policies. In more practical ways Games organisers should be strongly encouraged to invest some sponsorship proceeds in a series of trusts and endowments to support sporting projects, communities and individuals from deprived backgrounds. Many sports bodies, from table-tennis associations to athletics and football clubs, already possess good working relationships and networks within deprived communities and represent an existing resource that can be developed and promoted. Such expansion would not only benefit agencies that support and nurture grassroots sport but also directly benefit young people who are often marginal players within mainstream development programmes.

An Olympic Games also provides an opportunity to increase the profile of sporting events for people with disabilities who have long been marginalised in regeneration and development projects. As Edwards (2003:179) argues: 'the government does not see disabled people as part of the urban problem, despite the exclusion they experience and their over-representation in deprived areas'. A Paralympic Games has the potential to act as a both a symbolic event that challenges dominant negative perceptions of those with disabilities and as an opportunity to create new programmes that break down barriers of social exclusion. Initiatives that tackle the needs of disabled groups in and around Games' sites could be implemented along with national programmes that expand the availability of specialised sporting and training facilities. By highlighting the problems currently faced by such groups and acting as a catalyst for community-targeted development programmes, an Olympic Games could create a direct and very powerful social legacy.

The Games could also be used to up-grade infrastructure networks across London's East End. The relatively poor state of the transport network in the area is well known and arguably exaggerated. What is less publicised is the poor state of housing, the legacies of contamination on former industrial sites, and the dilapidated state of 'hidden' infrastructure, such as water systems and communications networks. As argued in Chapter 1, in these areas an Olympic Games could act as a focus for significant new investment. For example, Barcelona's e-networks were given a significant boost by the 1992 Games in ways that probably would not have occurred without it. In Sydney a number of disused, heavily polluted sites have become role models for environmentally-sensitive, attractively-designed urban regeneration, again as a direct spin-off from investments associated with the Games. Some projects are planned for East London, such as environmental improvements in the Lower Lea Valley. But the Games could be used to underpin other projects such as a major expansion in IT infrastructure networks (including Broadband access) that would help tackle the digital divide that excludes poorer communities from many of the benefits of e-networks, whilst also making the area increasingly attractive to investors and incomers. A range of Section 106 planning agreements and housing association-led projects could, with local input, identify areas of social need and draw resources into the area from central government and private developers to directly tackle poor quality housing provision.

In addition, the organisers and the Government need to learn from other cities, such as Manchester, where a failure to attract the

Olympic Games did not mean that all proposed infrastructure projects were abandoned. As Harding *et al* (2004:46) point out the failure to attract the 1996 and 2000 Olympic Games was paradoxically the catalyst 'on which much of the subsequent success rested'. The city benefited from new sports facilities and the bidding process brought forward new investments in its transport and tourism infrastructure. Regeneration 'plans' do exist in the event of failed London Bid but these have not been widely publicised as they may be perceived to indicate a 'lack of confidence' in the Bid's prospects of success. This should not be allowed to happen as the Olympic Games should be seen as complementary to existing programmes and act as a significant opportunity to generate new forms of development that meet local expectations as well as bringing about much needed environmental and property regeneration. Regeneration should not be dependent on the lottery that is the Olympic Games bidding process.

Conclusion

This chapter has argued that the social legacies of an Olympic Games will be critically dependent on the ways in which it is embedded into a wider set of strategic, well resourced policy agendas. Its ambitions must be couched in modest terms if it is not to disappoint and organisers need to think laterally about the multiple impacts that can result from such events. At the same time it must not draw investment away from bottom-up, grassroots sporting and community organisations and it needs to build on existing strengths and capacities in the surrounding areas. That having been said, with enough political will the 2012 Bid could represent a key moment in the broader politics of regeneration and economic development in the UK by challenging us to think about the type of London that we want to create and the relationship that the capital should have with the rest of the country. London is a very divided city. Nowhere in western Europe matches its extremes of cheek-by-jowl affluence and deprivation and an Olympic Games could play a part in changing the physical and social infrastructure of some of its poorest neighbourhoods. As this chapter has argued this can only be achieved if local knowledge and skills are embraced and championed by those delivering a 2012 Games, not put to one side as has been the tendency of past projects. Resources will need to be set aside to develop community capacities and ensure that the benefits flow from a Games into local communities, whilst minimising the costs. Thought also needs to be given to the effects that may result in other regions. One legacy could be that a Games further increases the attraction of London as a centre for young, skilled people from the rest of UK and beyond and plays a part in increasing uneven development. Olympic-driven growth in the London area will, therefore, have to be counterbalanced by development elsewhere.[10]

Whether or not the 2012 Games do come to London the bidding process has already generated debate and thinking over what role East London could and should play in the development of London and the South East. It has drawn attention to the significant development opportunities offered by the area and the socioeconomic needs of its residents. If the Games goes ahead then its social impacts will depend on the types of projects that are put in place alongside the sporting infrastructure. The lessons of earlier rounds of flagship and sporting event-led regeneration indicate that a strategically thought through combination of local initiatives and mainstream government programmes will be required to generate a progressive social legacy. Within the East End the Games will not be seen as a success unless they boost local employment, improve the availability of affordable and social housing, kick-start investment in local educational and health services and infrastructure, improve transport connections, and develop networks of community consultation and ownership of development agendas. To implement such a programme will require significant central government backing and a carefully regulated relationship with private sector investors. Too often in the UK the social legacies of regeneration have been an afterthought. The Olympic Games could act as a focus for a more rounded form of regeneration, drawing on lessons from past events and creating its own, alternative example of best practice. It the long run it is by acting as a role model for progressive regeneration that a London Games could have its greatest social legacy.

3 Making the Games Work

A sustainable employment legacy

Martin Crookston

3 Making the Games Work
A sustainable employment legacy
Martin Crookston

The 2012 Olympic Games, if they were to be held in London, would be primarily held in a part of the metropolis that is part of the justification for bidding. That is to say: in the East End, with its long-term problems of deprivation, economic underperformance and stigma – not in one or more or our famous great sporting locations, whether Wembley (the main home of the 1948 Olympics), Wimbledon, or Lords.[1] And specifically, in the Lower Lea Valley: which the last two decades of urban regeneration has done rather less to change than in say Docklands, Paddington or Battersea.

So economic change, regeneration and employment opportunity are tightly bound in to the thinking about where and how the UK Bid is approached. This was probably a Barcelona invention – along with 'Olympics as city re-branding' and 'Olympics interwoven with cultural appeal'. Because of this approach, and the way it is more or less taken for granted by policy-makers, there is a lot of pressure on the Bid Team to ensure that the Games (if won, of course) do in fact deliver a raft of such benefits.

This chapter will briefly outline what the approach is to securing the employment legacy, provide a view on how likely the sought-for benefits are, and then sketch out some of the priorities for a successful Bid in these terms.

The scale of the challenge – what are we trying to achieve?

The lead responsibility for securing the employment legacy lies with the London Development Agency (LDA). They see the challenge as maximising the benefits for local people: in the construction phase, during a Games, and in the 'legacy' post-Games period. The range of outcomes sought is ambitious – a more competitive and responsive labour market; capitalising on key growth sectors; a catalyst for regeneration in the Lower Lea Valley; and, slightly ambiguously (because it makes it less clear what the focus of the effort actually is), spreading opportunities across London and beyond to the regions (LDA 2004).

The LDA identify the challenges they face as being high unemployment, low economic activity, inequality of opportunity, a multicultural population with different needs and aspirations, and a need to learn the lessons of the past: especially, presumably, from Docklands, with its tendency to go for development *per se* and think about the consequences and beneficiaries afterwards.

As demonstrated in Chapter 1, unemployment (quite high) and deprivation (very high) are undoubtedly serious issues in East London and the Lower Lea Valley boroughs. Furthermore, the employment rates are low, as they are in the London labour market as a whole. However, this is not really because there are not sufficient jobs – after all, the Lower Lea Valley is about ten kilometres from the biggest concentration (1.2 million) of jobs in North West Europe, just a few stops away on the London Underground between Bank and Marble Arch stations. The low employment rate is not, therefore, solely due to a low demand for labour. Rather, social factors lie behind the problem (some on the 'supply side', like lack of skills or labour-market readiness, some on the 'demand side', like recruiting practices and stigmatisation). From which it follows that just creating jobs via an Olympic Games would not necessarily be a very cost-effective strategy. Significant complementary measures will be needed as well.

The LDA's Skills & Employment Directorate recognise this and have a threefold strategy to tackle it:

■ Understanding demand – what sort of jobs, in what sectors, at what skill levels

■ Developing capacity – including a skills assessment of the Lower Lea Valley area workforce

- Tackling barriers to work – improving routes into work through a range of support programmes, local labour agreements, using the 'volunteering' programme idea which seems to have been a success in Sydney.

The overall regeneration effort for the Lower Lea Valley is targeting the creation of 1,000 new businesses, 30,000 new homes, and 40,000 new jobs (Williams 2004). With a successful Bid there would be a two hundred-hectare Olympic Park at the heart of the Lower Lea Valley, close to the major transport hub and Channel Tunnel Rail station at Stratford, and with stadia and other sports venues which would all have a clear post-Games legacy plan.

With any major and ambitious scheme like this, there is inevitably an issue of employment loss and thus of the net gains being lower than the gross potential. There would be a considerable industrial relocation effort required, and over quite a concentrated period, if the Bid were successful. It is true that all such major regeneration efforts impose this need, because the persistence of low-value industrial or storage activities is often a direct symptom of market failure in the locality. Nevertheless, the time pressures of an Olympic Games effort would be very much more compressed than for a conventional regeneration/relocation process, even on the scale of Docklands at its mid-80s peak. The danger would be commensurately greater that businesses were extinguished rather than relocated, because there simply was not time to go through all the time-consuming processes (also see Chapter 2).

A successful 2012 Bid would of course throw into sharp focus a specific set of businesses and skills which would be required and which could benefit. They range across the major sectors, and include:

Production industries
Particular opportunities here are in food and drink production, merchandising and supplies and machinery for the construction and maintenance effort. These sectors are nationally and internationally

traded, and are one of the main ways the rest of the country might benefit in employment terms from a successful Bid. For London, there may be potential employment gains, providing the Games organisation and the LDA work closely with supply chains and industry groupings.

Services

Catering, accommodation, retail, hosting/reception, translation/interpreting, security and general office support are the biggest opportunities here. These are the big direct and indirect employment sectors, with a wide range of skill levels and with the possibility of getting local people, especially young people, interested, enthused and trained – the Games as a route for many into new opportunity even from a low base. A special aspect of this is in relation to disabled people. The combination of Olympics and Paralympics gives unusual prominence to the issues of disability and access, and ought to be capable of giving leverage to specially-designed programmes to attract disabled people, train them and deploy them. However, getting the most out of all these kinds of jobs will need really positive, proactive policy programmes: otherwise the Games will be staffed entirely by cheery, competent Kiwis and Aussies, with minimal East End participation.

London tourism will be a big beneficiary as an industry and as a set of businesses. The hotel stock will cope without creating much new capacity or employment, and it seems very unlikely that new attractions of London-wide significance will be created by the Olympic Games. A visitor focus needs critical mass, as has been painstakingly created in London's new visitor hub on the South Bank. It must be remembered that the South Bank is right next to Central London and its established visitor circuits; even a great cluster of attractions like Greenwich only attracts a third of the numbers that like-for-like attractions in Central London do (ETC Research and Intelligence 2000). So, therefore, the Lower Lea Valley is unlikely to become a significant new centre for tourist activity.

Construction

There are a range of opportunities here, from highly-specialised professionals through skilled tradespeople, to general labouring. There is a danger that this will be much more of a project-development problem than an employment opportunity – given the extreme tightness of the building labour market, the existence of other major developments competing for that scarce supply, and the slowness and inadequacy of recruitment and training processes in this fragmented industry. In theory, a major, high-profile and publicly-supported scheme like the Olympics ought to be a focus for a concerted and sustained recruitment and training effort; and one which could provide direct opportunities for a wide range of local residents in the East End. There is sadly no evidence whatsoever so far of an integrated programme to try to respond. The Thames Gateway Construction Academy initiative, by the LDA and partners, is a worthy but essentially lightweight response to the major housing-driven programme in the sub-region. A significant challenge will be to create a more meaningful response in the gap between a winning Bid announcement and the need to start building. This is not, however, by any means an easy task.

Transport

Specifically, transport for competitors, officials, and visitors, over and above what the basic London transport systems will carry daily. Much has been made of this, and the supposed lack of necessary infrastructure investment, particularly by the navel-gazing British, but in fact the capacity at Stratford is far greater than at most host-city focal points, and the additional transport needed will mostly be supplied by drivers of various sizes of bus from limo to coach; probably requiring some temporary recruitment, but not out of line with other major events.

An important issue, discussed later in the chapter, is how much of this potential is capable of being harnessed under both the 'Win' and 'Lose' scenarios. Many of the activities, clearly, are simply not going to happen if the 2012 Olympic Games goes to another Candidate City instead. An obvious instance would be the 'extra drivers' example sketched out above. Others, however, might be sectors and activities where even the Bid could be the trigger for a programme, which might be sustained under the 'no-Games' scenario. Construction ought to be in this category but, especially given the reservations over the Thames Gateway Construction Academy, will require significant new thinking. At its most successful, the effort for an Olympic Games could help open doors for thousands of local people, who would otherwise struggle to compete in the increasingly-sophisticated London labour market, especially in some of these opportunity sectors. The programmes to realise this aim would, however, need to be very sophisticated as well.

The scale of the possible – what might an Olympics offer?

These are ambitious aims, and they rely on complex interactions in a field (physical regeneration's leverage through to employment and poverty reduction) where our record has been quite patchy (for further discussion, see Chapter 2). How likely is it all to happen?

We can perhaps start at the negative end and work towards the positive. The main negative, of course, is the probability of an unsuccessful Bid. The LDA argue that they have a 'dual scenario', with strategies for whether London gets the 2012 Olympic Games or not, and that the catalytic effect can still be used for regeneration even if another Candidate City wins. This chapter later argues that the 'focus' benefits of the Bid are an important thing to concentrate on. But that aside, a theme running through this book is the need to be realistic: London is one of five Candidate Cities and if the Games do not come, many of the claimed benefits probably will not either.

Even assuming a successful Bid, there is what one might call the 'null hypothesis' about the Olympic Games, which could be summarised as:

■ It is a two-week event, and events have little effect on long-run processes, particularly established and sticky ones like unemployment and deprivation.

- Although it is a world event, London is already a 'world city', with a global tourism reach and a range of attractions wider even than those of New York or Paris. The effect of the Olympic Games on its profile is completely different in scale or value to its effect on an Atlanta or even a Barcelona.

- Whilst quite a significant economic sector, sport is not a big industry, with spending far below that of other major leisure activities, and the actual scale of activity will be quite small in the context of London's economy and society.

- Sport spending is anyway mainly on sports clothing and trainers (most of which is made outside the UK) and not on the activity itself.

There is quite a lot of evidence to support a cautious view. David Green at the University of British Columbia looked at the record of the Winter Games. Green's downbeat conclusion: 'The experience of Lake Placid, Calgary and Salt Lake City tells us that we should expect about 10,000 person-years of employment, equivalent to about 1,400 new jobs lasting seven years. Moreover [this is] offset by a reduction in employment after the Games [because of] limited government capital budgets.' (2003)

Stefan Szymanski at Imperial College is similarly sceptical. Taking the arguments about extra trade being generated, Szymanski argues, in a point of some relevance for the London accommodation industry as well as more generally: 'Business can take advantage of extra profits, but the question is to what extent that represents a stimulus to the local economy. If a hotel is full and there is a big increase in demand because of the Games, there could only be a real increase in local economic activity if the owners build another hotel.' (Szymanski 2002a) Szymanski also produces a graph of France's tourism statistics for the years either side of the 1998 World Cup in which no effect is visible at all (see Figure 3.1).

Estimates from promoters, as one might expect, make the position look rather more promising. The Japan-Korea World Cup of 2002

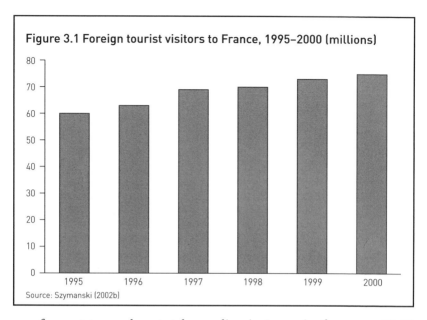

Figure 3.1 Foreign tourist visitors to France, 1995–2000 (millions)

Source: Szymanski (2002b)

was forecast to produce total spending in Japan in the range £2.65 billion to £6 billion, with 350,000 visitors (out of 750,000 to the two countries); as Szymanski (2002b) points out, the figure was still around 0.2 per cent of Japan's GDP.

Sydney 2000's Olympic Coordinating Authority (OCA) has produced an interesting range of analyses of the estimated economic effects (OCA 2002). Their estimate of the contribution over ten years to the Australian economy is £2.5 billion. This is an impressive figure, but the £250 million per year it implies should be compared with London's annual Gross Domestic Product of £165 billion. OCA estimate 100,000 new jobs nationally in Australia, and 110,000 Games-specific visitors – London's would undoubtedly be much higher than this. They attribute to the Olympics the Convention Bureau having won 210 events it would not otherwise have gained, attracting 250,000 delegates, and bringing £380 million into the regional economy (OCA 2002). Also hooked onto Olympics-related promotion was New South Wales's special NSW Investment 2000 programme: attributed are forty five investments, £200 million inward investments, and 1,150 jobs (OCA 2002). In addition, Olympics contracts for small businesses in NSW are claimed to have been worth £113 million. An *ex-post* economic analysis characterises the macro-economic impact as having been 'modest', but notes that accurate attribution of effects is particularly difficult over a period which was also affected by a new Sales Tax and a general economic slowdown (*Australian Special Events Industry Newsletter* 2002). These reports and estimates – from sceptical to positive – can be compared with the assessment by the Arup economic consultancy for the LDA. They place the possible benefit at a net gain to the UK economy of £82 million. However, they do also say that the downside risk could be as high as a net disbenefit of £145 million (Arup 2002).

The Tourism Society, a respected industry grouping, have held discussion meetings and open think-tank sessions with their membership about potential benefits and strategies. Their conclusions, based on other recent Games, are that over half the long-term net economic benefit of hosting the Games is from tourism; and that even though normal tourism is greatly disrupted during the periods surrounding the Games, in the two years before and after, the heightened international profile of the UK and London will have a strongly beneficial effect on demand for the UK as a holiday destination (Robinson 2003).

Thus it is apparent that the issue of the economic and employment benefit of a London 2012 Olympic Games is far from an open-and-shut case. Assuming, though, that there will be a significant number of new employment opportunities that might be exploited, there are four vital questions that must be addressed:

Can the Lower Lea Valley respond?

London's labour market is a large and fluid one, and there is no reason why jobs in an area should particularly be filled by existing residents of that area. Even the jobs with the lowest pay (so in theory most likely to be filled by locals with low travel costs) and the most anti-social hours are, in London, often filled by non-locals who are prepared to travel and compete. And further up the employment ladder, the better the jobs are, the more likely it is that those filling them are travelling in through low-employment areas every morning.

Can the immediately neighbouring and deprived wards really benefit?

Based on past recruitment priorities, the Lower Lea Valley's industries are currently as likely to recruit in the 'wider East End' (the diaspora that stretches out to Romford or Chingford) as they are in the nearby wards of Tower Hamlets or Hackney. This is not a uniquely East London feature – in Park Royal, too, on the A40 heading west, a surprising number of the predominantly blue-collar jobs are filled by

---

Box 3.1 The Minneapolis NET

We are looking to combine an over-arching training framework with a local orientation that could comprehensively meet the needs of both the unemployed and businesses who could hire them. One of the most interesting initiatives is the Minneapolis Neighbourhood Employment Network (NET) initiative. It provides a type of one-stop-shop facility for both employers and the unemployed. For over a decade, the NET has been assisting residents of Minneapolis, Minnesota, USA to find and keep jobs close to home.

The NET task force began by dividing the city into 10 geographical units, covering areas of the greatest need. Each area contains residents marginalised from the labour market, yet also small local employers or several large employers (in the case of the Lower Lea Valley, these employers could be existing or prospective). If a large employer does not exist in the area, then the area could be matched with a major employer in a nearby area.

The NET strategy is not just about helping people find jobs, but about helping to break down barriers to productive, successful employment. It has established itself as a link between job seekers, employers and the multitude of education, training and social programmes operating in Minneapolis. The barriers range from illiteracy to a lack of reliable transportation, from limited skills and low esteem, to lack of childcare. These diverse barriers necessitate a flexible approach to the provision of training services.

---

workers commuting in from outer suburbia, and not by people from the surrounding estates like White City, Chalkhill, or South Acton (Llewelyn-Davies with LSE 2000). Some of this is attributable to hiring practices (advertising in the Romford paper, but not the *East London Advertiser*); some of course to absence of skills, or fluent English, or labour-market/basic workplace readiness; and some to the realities of how people really get work. DfES-commissioned research by Thom and Convery (2003) indicates that the single largest method by which people secure new employment in London is via word-of-mouth, thus excluding those not already in personal-contact circuits, whether in pubs, families or supermarket queues.[2] One interesting initiative, in Minneapolis, the NET, has sought to link specific employers with specific estates, to help make the links that get people in deprived areas to opportunities directly rather than through various second-hand procedures.

What about the wider East End and Inner London?

It is not just the immediate edges of the Lower Lea Valley (Bow, Stratford, Homerton, Leyton etc) that are of concern, of course. This inner focal area forms part of an arc of boroughs, from Lambeth in the inner south round to Islington in the inner north, which contains many of Britain's top ten local authority areas along the Index of Multiple Deprivation – up there with Easington, and Glasgow (ONS 2004). In this sense, the Lower Lea Valley, and the Olympic Park, sit within an attempt to link in Inner North East London to the Growth Area strategy for the London-Stansted-Cambridge corridor.[3] Imaginative masterplanning and 'place-making' are attempts to change the supply side to compete for some of that growth: but again, the devil is in the detail of how major new development can be turned into real local benefit.

What **are** the micro-economic processes that must be influenced by the effort the LDA is leading?

This brings us back to the LDA's issues of understanding demand, developing capacity and tackling barriers. Experience by now surely tells us that it is not enough to work on the labour demand side by creating the big schemes (whether an Olympic Games or Canary Wharf) and to work on the supply side by generalised or top-down responses (generic training programmes, the proposed Construction Academy, formal equal opportunity recruitment, sectoral studies of industries with potential etc). We need to know who is hiring who, and how; what businesses are trading with what businesses; who (locally) is selling the goods and services that might benefit from the Bid and the Games, and are they interested in growing those businesses. We need specific, location-targeted programmes. Examples of innovative ideas that should be drawn upon are barrier-breaking ideas like the Minneapolis NET (Box 3.1) and regional good practice like Greenwich's local-labour agreements for the Greenwich Peninsula and Woolwich Arsenal. It is also important local businesses are worked with now to understand their trading patterns and place in the supply chain well before the orders associated with a 2012 Olympic Games come.

A sustainable employment legacy?

What then might a sustainable employment legacy mean? What might the (dread word) targets be? The impacts we are looking for are:

- Many more jobs than just a few hundred temporary assistants at a two-week party.

- A high proportion of that employment taken by people already resident in the short-bus-journey catchment of the Olympic Games site – not just a few residual security or driving jobs.

- That new employment connected to training adds to people's employment prospects long term.

- New work created in businesses in and around the East End, capturing locally some of the spending that the event will generate.

Can these be quantified better than qualitative assessments such as 'many more', 'high proportion' and 'some'? Not here or yet – that depends on knowing more than we do at present about the local economy and labour markets, which means survey-based research. For the impacts to be sustainable beyond the closing ceremony, there need to be both focused programmes to link opportunities to needs, and imaginative and different ways of reaching out to trigger new linkages.

The focus of programmes must be on person-to-person links. This applies in several senses:

- Employer/employer group to individual people/local estate level bodies, à la Minneapolis NET

- Person-specific training with a job prospect in view

- Responses which deal with perceived barriers to employment, whether inadequate and expensive childcare or unsafe-feeling walk routes to work – both of which featured at least as high up some of the Park Royal responses, for example, as skills issues.

It is clear that top-down training programmes and a reliance on a trickle-down and out of benefits will not be enough. Getting people into jobs, and supporting them with the skills and wider knowledge that equips them for the rest of the London labour market, is the twin underlying aim.

Imaginative recruitment strategies, combined with training, could include major national employers using an Olympic Games as a deliberate tool to target and interest (say) young people in the East End. Some possible examples for a 2012 Games are: the BBC and television companies offering scholarships into journalism or production; the major hotel operators sponsoring management traineeships; and the big construction groups marketing real skilled-trade apprenticeships to communities where young people have traditionally not known what the prospects were within the construction sector. Without this sort of deliberate spin, the various industries will more or less cope (they are very big and very flexible after all) and the opportunities are likely to be missed.

In the immortal words of Comrade V.I. Ulyanov (aka Lenin) in his seminal pamphlet *What Is To Be Done?*, 'what specific actions are needed?' They seem to fall under four main headings:

Research
We do need to know more, in much more detail, in order to inform properly-targeted programmes. The surveys and analysis must be about local people's skills, aspirations and perceived barriers; about real-life processes of recruitment and contracting; about the hinterland's businesses and their ability (and wish) to respond to the potential an Olympic Games can bring; and about best-practice and experience in other boroughs, cities and countries. That in turn means understanding better what the experience of Sydney 2000, Manchester's Commonwealth Games and other Games have taught us about the economic opportunities and the best ways of capturing them.

Person-to-person programmes and linkages
The LDA, Learning and Skills Councils and their multitude of partners must get very, very local: residents on the Barley Mow Estate need to be got talking to the personnel manager at Percy Dalton's Famous Peanuts, not expected just to read bus-shelter ads about courses in hairdressing or computers at the local FE College.

Training focus, which must continually be on 'the Olympics and beyond'
Training cannot simply focus on the Games-only needs. An example of this might be translation and interpreting, where the language ability/skill itself will be far less significant than the knowledge gained about how to use it, deploy it, sell it, and transfer it from one language to another.

Agencies
The LDA have the lead role, but it is unrealistic to see them as responding to all these needs – even in partnership with other (already-stretched) agencies. We are dealing here with at least two

important sectors which pose special difficulties: construction, where the Government has now spent six years and two Task Forces trying to change the quantity and quality of the response, to little visible effect; and hotels and tourism, which is traditionally an easy-in, easy-out industry where low cost responses and low training investment have tended (though not uniformly) to be characteristic. The Olympic Games Bid does actually offer an opportunity to create a special agency which takes these efforts and applies them to one specific area and one specific set of projects. This could well be a more fruitful route than that tried to date: that is to say, generalised nation-wide schemes, and ministerial exhortation. That would mean that the LDA would need national government support (ODPM and/or DTI) and also genuine business and trade-union engagement.

Back then, finally, to the win/lose conundrum, and the 'dual scenario'. To get the most out of the potential, we have to start now, and act exactly as though the UK Bid is going to win. Otherwise, not only will the event not be ready in time, but the local linkages will not be maximised and the probability will grow of it all being a last-minute, quick-fix, agency-hired set of employment responses – with no sustained legacy at all except in Blue Arrow's results.

Yet equally, we have act as though the UK Bid is not going to win: not just because of the balance of probability, but also because it is crucial that the package of actions should still be credible, useful and meaningful to local people and businesses if another Candidate City wins the race to host the 2012 Games on 6 July 2005.

So the employment effort has to be organised as though it was all going to happen anyway – which it must, and which is of course partly a reflection of the fact that the Olympic Games Bid is a part but not all of the wider regeneration response to the problems and opportunities of the Lower Lea Valley.

It has a more serious practical aspect, which is one of timing. Any programmes that are designed from now on – which they must be, as is argued above – have to be focused and argued primarily in relation to the Bid. The programmes have to be credible and persuasive to the International Olympic Committee in terms, principally, of being part of the consensus-building, as well as coping strategies. But suddenly, in July 2005, they may have to be equally believable in terms of a non-Olympic Games strategy. Suddenly, merchandising will not matter, neither will competitor transport and block hotel-booking capacity for officials. Under this unfortunate scenario, any training, recruitment or procurement plans or supply-chain negotiations aimed at such things will look like a wrong call. So all the programmes have to be tested in terms of their 'exit' credibility and usefulness, whilst at the same time containing the flexibility to respond very fast indeed if it is Mayor Livingstone who punches the air on 6 July next year.

Conclusion

The development and activity associated with hosting an Olympic Games can provide employment opportunities across a number of sectors. But a range of programmes and initiatives will be required if these are to provide sustainable employment for the local communities of East London. There is a significant and persistent deprivation and employment problem in East London, and hosting an Olympic Games cannot solve this on its own. Converting physical regeneration into local economic benefit is always very complex and the Olympics is an especially complicated way of doing it. In fact, the direct economic effects of the Olympic Games can be frequently overestimated.

Providing employment benefits to the local residents is not simply a question of creating new jobs. If the Olympic Games is to have a positive effect on the persistently high unemployment rates within East London then a range of supply-side measures are required. These must be based upon a detailed understanding of individuals' needs and the hiring activities of employers. This will require significant effort and only strengthens the case for the need to act immediately. If London wins the race to host the Games, we must hit the ground running.

4 Is Green the New Gold?
A sustainable Games for London

Roger Levett

4 Is Green the New Gold?
A sustainable Games for London
Roger Levett

Previous Games, notably Sydney, have already set impressive standards on many aspects of environmental performance. But growing recognition of the gravity of human environmental impacts and of the interdependence of environmental, social and economic aims challenges future Olympiads to raise their game. London can, and should, at least equal what has already been achieved. But London offers new opportunities as well as constraints of its own.

This paper outlines how an ambitious approach to sustainability can not only provide a better setting for the sporting heart of a London Olympiad, and reduce risks to its success, but could also re-energise the Games' role as an icon of human aspiration and endeavour. The International Olympic Commission (IOC), Environment Commission's strapline is: 'promoting Olympic Games that respect the environment and meet the requirements of sustainable development.' This statement is general enough to be interpreted in a range of ways. But further down the web page there is a much stronger statement: 'The aim is not just to ensure that holding the Games has no negative net impact on the environment, but also to try to improve the environment and leave behind a positive green legacy.'

Leave aside the 'positive green legacy' for now: is the basic aim – the 'not just to ensure that holding the Games has no negative net impact on the environment' bit – not already impossibly ambitious? How can an event that in its very nature involves buildings on the most heroic scale, infrastructure and services to match, and vast numbers of people coming from the ends of the earth to be concentrated intensely together in one place, possibly avoid big impacts on the environment? Would a serious attempt to live up to this commitment not make the Games impossible in anything like the form we are used to?

This chapter will identify a number of the opportunities and challenges that a London 2012 presents and outline how meeting the seemingly impossible challenge identified above could be met.

How to achieve 'no negative net impact on the environment'

The word 'net' offers a clue. 'No negative net impact' could be achieved if positive impacts achieved through the Games could offset negative ones. But environmental impacts are notoriously varied and disparate. There is no objective or agreed 'conversion rate' according to which we could say how much greenhouse gas emissions would be justified to achieve a certain amount of contaminated land cleanup, or how much impact on biodiversity would be acceptable to provide so much more recreational access. Indeed even talking about trade-offs in such a coldly calculating way feels uncomfortable.

The problem can be avoided if we limit offsetting to impacts of the same kind. From the planet's point of view, some extra greenhouse gas emissions (say from people flying to London) could be fully and satisfactorily offset by anything that reduces greenhouse emissions by the same amount – things as varied as buses that reduce car use in Birmingham, solar panels in Freiburg or replanting rainforest in Brazil. Only an impact that matters cumulatively at the level of the whole planet can be substituted anywhere on the planet in this way. Other impacts must be offset at the same level they are felt at. So, for example, loss of newt habitat can be replaced by creation of new newt habitat within the same area where newts are scarce; loss of recreational access to greenspace can be made up for by providing new access equally accessible and enjoyable to the people affected.

Of course the substitutions have to be actually made, and not be things that would have happened anyway. They have to match whatever is lost in quality as well as quantity, and cover all the significant negative impacts. For example, if an area in the Lower Lea Valley built on for the Olympics has recreational, biodiversity and water management value, then to achieve 'no net negative impact' we have to accommodate the recreational uses and species populations affected and provide an alternative way to manage the water.

This may seem daunting. However, only environmental benefits and services which are both important and scarce need to be offset. Substitutions for different impacts do not necessarily have to be in the same place as each other. Indeed the substitute does not even need to be the same physical kind of thing: what matters is that it makes up for the benefit lost. Loss to development of a patch of land does not have to be substituted by provision of another patch of land: often the benefits lost can be recouped by cleverer management of other areas to add to the benefits they provide.

Of course avoiding or minimising damage in the first place is more elegant and foolproof, and usually simpler and cheaper, than implementing substitutions. In any case some environmental qualities are in their nature not substitutable (for example historic buildings and sites). Others are so difficult or slow to replace that for practical purposes they must be treated as non-substitutable. The ecological richness of ancient woodland takes at least five hundred years to develop. In principle we can create new ancient woodland – but we would have had to have started in Tudor times to have it ready for the 2012 Olympics.

How could the twin principles of first avoiding/minimising and then substituting for environmental impacts be applied to the Olympics in London? The rest of this section considers some of the biggest impacts.

Climate change

Climate change caused by greenhouse gas emissions is now clearly the biggest environmental threat to future human welfare and is an issue a London Olympics must take seriously.

Reduction – Air travel

Air travel is one of the most carbon-intense activities people can carry out. The extra air travel generated by the Games is likely to dwarf all their other environmental impacts. The top priority for any Games to be taken seriously for sustainability must therefore be to minimise their air travel intensity. London's Bid has a big potential opportunity here: the Lower Lea Valley is near Stratford station, which is connected via the Channel Tunnel high speed link to the Western European high speed rail system. It would be physically possible for most Olympic participants and spectators from all over Europe to come to a London Olympics by rail in under a day's travel time. High speed trains could run direct to Stratford from, for example, Amsterdam, Copenhagen, Berlin, Vienna, Zurich, Munich, Milan, Lyon, Barcelona and Madrid. A great deal of planning and organisation would be needed to make this possible, but very little additional physical infrastructure. London should make a commitment to no additional short haul flights into London. This could allow for some Games visitors to fly in, but this would need to be balanced by non-Olympic air travellers switching to rail.

For people prepared to spend days rather than hours travelling, it is physically possible to get to London by rail from much of Asia. By 2012, the next generation of long rail tunnels (including links between European and Asian Turkey under the Bosporus, and under the Straits of Gibraltar connecting Europe with West and South Africa) may have significantly increased the ease and speed of intercontinental rail travel. The expansion of cruise shipping re-creates the potential capacity to lay on comfortable and enjoyable sea travel to the Olympics which has been lacking since air travel supplanted sea four decades ago.

The Olympics creates the critical mass of enough people all wanting to go to the same place at the same time to make arranging some long distance trains and ships potentially viable. Perhaps even more importantly, the Olympics' sense of an exceptional occasion on which the whole human family takes time out from 'business as usual' to do something special together could make people open to travel choices they would not normally consider. (This 'exceptionalness' point will be returned to later).

Reduction – Buildings and sporting venues
Buildings and sporting venues will also be a major source of greenhouse gas emissions, in their construction, use both during and after the Games, any adaptation needed for afteruse and eventual decommissioning. Methods for minimising climate change impacts at all these stages are already well understood:

In construction:

- Reuse and adapt existing buildings in preference to replacement and new build where possible;

- Use reclaimed materials;

- Source all materials as locally as possible; transport by water and rail as much as possible.

- Use materials with high-embodied energy (metal, glass, cement, polymers) sparingly.

In use:

- Design to stay comfortable under the widest range of possible weather and other use conditions with the least use of building services such as mechanical heating/cooling/air conditioning, lifts, artificial lighting.

- Use natural heating/cooling, lighting, ventilation as much as possible.

- Make any necessary building services and appliances energy-efficient, not oversized, and with controls that use them economically.

In adaptation/decommissioning:

- Make spaces as versatile and adaptable as possible to minimise the physical changes needed for adaptation.

- Build in a modular way to make dismantling and remodelling easy.

- Design to facilitate eventual separation, reclamation and reuse of structural elements and materials.

Different objectives often trade off against each other. For example, high embodied-energy materials such as steel open up design possibilities that may increase energy efficiency in use or adaptability; making buildings suitable for a wider range of uses may result in a less good fit for any one use, and so on. The special nature of the Olympic requirement will also limit how far some of these can be taken. Providing the best possible settings for sport must take top priority. Even London will not be able to supply a complete set of Olympic-class sporting venues from its existing building stock, or use them all afterwards without adaptation. Media and public attention will focus on the big 'set piece' sporting venues, so getting the best possible energy performance in these will be symbolically important. But arguably the biggest opportunity to make a lasting difference will come from the large volume of buildings that will be commissioned or used by the Olympics, but for 'normal' uses that will also continue after the Games: housing, offices, shops; catering kitchens, restaurants and bars; conference, meeting and reception rooms; broadcast studios; stores and workshops; stations, bus garages and so on.

Thanks to a wealth of inspiring pilot and demonstration buildings, we now know how to build a range of housing and other building types which do their jobs well while needing only a fraction of current normal energy input. There is no technical mystery about achieving a step change in energy efficiency in buildings. For example BedZed (Beddington Zero Energy Development) offers a prototype for an Olympic village with minimal greenhouse emissions (and outstanding performance on a range of other environmental impacts too). The barriers instead are financial, cultural and institutional. Building Regulations still set only unambitious energy efficiency levels, only apply to some buildings, and ignore many factors that influence energy actually used. The building industry is notoriously conservative, and with a few heroic exceptions does only the minimum required by law.

The UK's really outstanding demonstration projects like BedZed are the achievement of exceptional people driven by personal commitment, often having to struggle hard against regulations and established ways of doing things. Cost is also a problem. There is still plenty of 'low hanging fruit' – opportunities to save ten per cent, twenty per cent, thirty per cent of energy with no additional cost, or even saving money, simply through a bit more care and attention in the design and construction process. But energy is so cheap, and the markets in goods and services needed for really high performance so undeveloped in the UK, that costs often rise unacceptably well before all technically feasible energy saving measures have been applied. The issue of implementation will be returned to later.

Substitution

Even with all possible reduction measures the Games will still have a substantial greenhouse gas 'bubble'. As already pointed out, the principle of like for like substitution would allow this to be offset by anything that reduced greenhouse gas emissions anywhere in the world. The London Olympics could therefore simply buy the right amount of abatement from companies already offering it. However the amount needed opens up an opportunity to do something more inspiring and aspirational. For example an Olympic greenhouse gas reserve could be established, perhaps producing an endowment of carbon sequestration that could provide offsets for future Games. The size of reserve needed to offset just a brief event involving only a tiny fraction of the world's population once every four years would provide a sobering reminder of the scale of overconsumption.

Water resources

England is a very cloudy country, but (contrary to general belief) not very wet. The South East, where rainfall is lowest (East Anglia is classified as 'semi arid') and population densest, has one of the highest rates of exploitation of water resources in Europe. Climate change is already increasing demand and reducing supply, and this is likely to worsen. Thames Water has already announced plans to build a reverse osmosis desalination plant in the Thames estuary. The process is highly energy intensive; Thames would intend to run it only as a stopgap during periods of shortage. However the fact that such a desperate measure is under serious consideration is a measure of the gravity of the problem.

Reduction

As with energy, technologies for dramatically reducing consumption of piped water are already well proven. Simple methods such as spray heads on taps and showers, showers as an alternative to baths, low flush and duel flush toilets, and water-efficient washing machines and dishwashers, can achieve big reductions. Large-scale developments increase the practicality and cost-effectiveness of measures such as collecting rainwater for flushing and washing, or even filtering it to drinking standard, reusing water for lower grade uses (e.g. rinse water from a laundry for flushing, washing the next batch of washing or irrigation), waterless composting toilets, and regenerating water using reed beds or wetlands. These should all be exploited to the full.

Substitution

However, as with energy, the Games facilities will probably impose substantial extra piped water demand even if after all efficiency technologies and opportunities for collecting rainwater and such like are taken. As with energy, this can be offset by reductions elsewhere. However they would have to be in the same river catchment as the extra demand. One way to do this would be by helping other London businesses or households to reduce water consumption. Putting bricks in a million London loo cisterns is perhaps not the most exalted way to welcome the Games but could make an important point.

Transport in London

Transport to and from the Games has already been discussed under greenhouse emissions above. Transport within London is also a major impact. All motorised transport, but especially cars, contribute significantly to greenhouse emissions. Traffic is the main source of air and noise pollution in London. Roads, car parks and other motoring provision take up large areas of land, and roads sever communities, but despite this there is still frequent congestion.

Reduction

Given how close to gridlock London often is already, minimising Games traffic would not only be good for the environment, it would also be prudent to reduce the risk that extra loading from the Games would precipitate an embarrassing (indeed humiliating) breakdown. The Sydney Games were car free for spectators. If that was possible in a country with even more of a car culture than the UK, longer distances, less developed public transport and more space available, it should be the minimum starting point for London. The IOC rule book requires host cities to lay on a fleet of cars for athletes and officials. It is hard to reconcile this requirement with the IOC's own sustainability aims. London should minimise the numbers involved, make greener alternatives, such as bicycles, available for athletes and officials to use, and ensure that the cars are as sustainable as possible, especially by using the smallest and simplest vehicles suitable for the purpose.

The best way to minimise local transport impacts will be to minimise the need to travel by locating the sporting venues and their associated accommodation and supporting facilities as close together as practicable given the constraints of using existing buildings and finding space for new ones in an intensively developed urban area. London 2012's Bid already takes this on with a highly compact proposal for the Lower Lea Valley site.

The second way is to make it as easy and attractive as possible for people to walk and cycle to, from and between Olympic venues. These modes offer personal freedom and flexibility with a fraction of space requirement of cars or taxis. A network of cycle expressways serving and linking Olympic venues, with large scale cycle parking, could be very good value for money in reducing the need for heavier transport infrastructure. Some of these issues are beyond the formal remit of the Bid and will require close cooperation with the surrounding five Olympic boroughs.

The third way is public transport. Being able to move large numbers of people around promptly, reliably and comfortably will be central to the success of the Games. The opportunity should be taken to showcase cleaner transport technologies.

Substitution

As with greenhouse emissions and water, the Olympics will still impose a big extra loading on transport in London even if the reduction measures outlined are pursued to the utmost. As with these, offsetting is possible – but again the relevant area for substitutions is different. The better public transport, walking and cycling facilities laid on for the Olympics should enable Londoners to use these modes more after the Games. However, this will not offset increased demand during the Games themselves. Most of the underground and surface rail system is already at or near capacity (if not actually beyond it) so it is unrealistic to expect it to carry more. Although the organisers are confident they have addressed the transport capacity issue through rail freight diversion measures for example, it should be remembered that buses can be increased relatively easily. Extra bus services throughout London could provide one way to offset the extra Olympic use as well as provide a permanent legacy in terms of extra bus capacity for London.

Delivery

What is special about the Olympics? Much of the discussion so far could apply to any very large development project. But the Olympics have some special features:

■ The Olympics are time critical. Everything necessary for the Games must be in place and fully working by the predetermined fortnight; there is no possibility of slippage or deferral. London must convince the IOC seven years in advance that it has the capacity to deliver to this standard.

- The Olympics is the most prestigious and visible, as well as big and complex, of international gatherings. Nations are judged by their performance hosting the Games.

- The bar rises, but never falls: each Olympiad is judged against the best that has been achieved before, not lower performers.

- The Olympics have an aura of specialness: of being an event out of the ordinary, an occasion when normal routines are suspended.

- The Olympics are a vehicle for ideals – of peace, brother/sister-hood, better relations between nations and groups – over and above sport.

These special characteristics make the environmental approaches summarised more necessary, more possible and more beneficial. This chapter now moves on to discuss the implications for how the environmental requirements could be delivered.

Delivery of the whole Olympic project

London will need to reassure the IOC that it has not only the enthusiasm and the resources but also the delivery processes and mechanisms to get everything built and working reliably on time. The IOC may compare the inordinate time it takes the UK to build infrastructure such as the Channel Tunnel rail link unfavourably with the fast, fuss-free way the French built the other end of the same link, and deliver other major projects in and around Paris, a competitor for 2012.

The IOC may not be reassured if London's delivery proposals emphasise mechanisms for involving the private sector – tendering, contracting, franchising and public-private partnerships – which have, instead of the efficiency improvements promised, tended to produce heavy bureaucratic/legal/consultancy overheads, delay, fragmentation, inflexibility, spiralling costs, poor performance, lack of accountability and a culture of litigation and buck-passing in a wide range of projects and programmes. It will be important to learn from past mistakes, and institute methods that achieve clear and simple accountability for delivering results, can redeploy resources rapidly when needed, and respond to problems, opportunities and changing circumstances quickly and decisively without a huge process of negotiating variations to contracts. 'Command and control' has become a term of denigration, but a strong element of it will be needed to ensure success here.

Sustainable communities in the Lower Lea Valley

The Lower Lea Valley, as part of the Thames Gateway, is at the southern end of the London-Stansted-Cambridge-Peterborough corridor which the Government has designated for major housing and business growth. The Games provides a tremendous opportunity to build housing, community facilities and infrastructure in this corridor to high environmental standards that will achieve the Government's professed aims for sustainable communities, and help answer serious concerns about the consistency of the planned growth with environmental constraints, notably climate change, water resources and biodiversity.

As highlighted earlier, the barriers to creating sustainable communities are not technical, but institutional, behavioural and financial. A cautionary tale comes from the experience of the Government's flagship 'Millennium Communities'. Greenwich Millennium Village was intended to be the first of a series of flagship projects demonstrating a 'step change' in environmental performance, speed and cost through good design and innovative construction techniques. Consortia led by large development companies were invited to bid competitively to design and build the Village. The process was dogged by delays and disputes; the original lead architects left the consortium in acrimonious circumstances; the buildings actually delivered fell far short of the environmental standards which had been a key element of the contract, but a level of actual performance only slightly better than routine good practice was accepted in order to get the housing built. By July 2004, websites for the next three designated Millennium Communities were reporting a great deal of masterplanning and community consultation activity, but apparently not a single new home yet built.

The Government's own research contrasted this market-led development model unfavourably with other approaches. For example, with the smaller policy-led rather than market-led projects in the UK (notably BedZed) and with pilot sustainable communities from abroad, notably Vauban in Freiburg where a social democratic development model with strong public interest and no role for large commercial developers, had achieved much better results. The following proposals draw on the lessons of this research.

Delivery requirements for environmental benefits

Achieving the level of environmental performance sketched in the first half of this chapter will require integration across different disciplines, market sectors, service providers and regulatory regimes. For example, a sustainable approach to energy would require:

■ Much higher energy efficiency standards for individual buildings than set in current building regulations.

■ Coordinated development of small scale green energy production including combined heat and power generators using biomass and wastes (digestion of organic material), with heat distribution pipes, integral to all development.

■ A requirement to buy heat and power only from the designated green energy suppliers, to provide an assured market.

■ Power and resources to set up greenhouse gas substitution projects offsite.

Sustainable transport would require a combination of carrots – excellent accessibility, good cycling, walking and public transport provision, car clubs – but also sticks such as car ownership bans or levies and road charging. It would also rely on non-transport measures such as local provision of services.

Delivering this would require a coordinated planning and implementation process. This would entail bending or breaking some current rules, but strengthening others. Key aspects would include:

Performance standards

The Government's new 'Code for Sustainable Building' is a welcome push in the right direction as it goes further than current building regulations, however it is not a substitute for mandatory standards. Performance standards for all Olympic-related construction should be set standards in terms of outcomes such as the amount of greenhouse gas emissions, piped water and motorised transport that will result, or improvements in biodiversity and leisure provision. Development needs to be designed to meet Olympic requirements first, but environmental performance in post-Games after-use should have more weight. For example, housing should be located for good access to public services that permanent residents will need even if the athletes, media people or spectators who will occupy it during the Games will not.

This will require overriding two current rules. First, that development masterplans and site briefs cannot set mandatory energy efficiency standards since this is covered by the Building Regulations. Second, that customers are free to change energy supplier at will.

Market and capacity development

This will be needed in order to persuade a notoriously conservative construction industry to use methods and technologies which, although proven and even routine elsewhere, are unfamiliar here, and therefore regarded as difficult or risky. Moreover there is currently a vicious circle. UK market demand for many building products and services with really high environmental performance is so small that they are often only available to special order, with long lead times, restricted ranged and/or unreliable quality. The resulting delays, uncertainties, inflexibility and high costs put off all but the most determined. Even they often resort to importing what they need specially from countries with better developed industries (often in Scandinavia) despite the high costs, both financial and environmental. This of course helps keep UK markets too small to be viable.

The Olympics offer the potential for a 'critical mass' of demand which could break out of the vicious circle, enabling British firms to build wide enough ranges of high environmental performance products at low enough prices to make them an attractive option for any 'quality' job. The same critical mass could help make low energy and other environmentally better approaches and methods part of the body of technical knowledge and competence that any good professional should have, rather than an arcane specialism developed by a few niche players to cater to a fringe market.

These changes could constitute an important positive green legacy, and help achieve Governmental and Mayoral objectives to develop a green technology industry for London. They will require extensive coordination with professional and trade bodies, training providers and economic development agencies to provide the training, capacity building and business support to equip London businesses to exploit the challenge. But kick-starting local providers will also depend on the Olympics being able to develop a stable collaborative, supportive relationship with potential green suppliers, nurturing and developing them over time. This will require a derogation from standard competitive tendering rules, which would otherwise probably result the London Olympics just sucking in more Scandinavian imports over the heads of a stagnating local industry.

On- and off-site substitutions as part of the development 'package'
'No negative net impact on the environment' can only be achieved if, after all efforts have been made to minimise impacts, remaining negative impacts can be offset by positive impacts of the same kind. Some of these offsets can or must, because of their nature, be provided very near the development site (for example recreational access or wildlife corridors). Others can best, or even only, be achieved elsewhere. The London Olympics would need the power to require, carry out, or pay others to carry out, activities anywhere in the world to achieve environmental substitution. This goes beyond current government guidance which seeks to limit planning obligations to activities directly related to the development site.

Continuing proactive engagement and interventions
These will need to be integrated with the Olympic development programme throughout its course, including:

■ Negotiation of derogations and changes to rules and procedures to permit the environmental standards and approaches outlined.

■ Studies to identify impacts requiring reduction and substitution. For some, such as energy and water, it is already obvious what the impacts are and how they can be measured, but for others, such as recreation and biodiversity, extensive consultation, careful collation of baseline data and analysis and interpretation will be needed.

■ Researching methods and options for avoiding, obviating or at least minimising the impacts, and working with those involved to make sure they are incorporated to the greatest possible extent in briefs and designs.

■ Defining the conditions which valid potential substitutions must meet.

■ Identifying places and ways that substitutions could actually be implemented, negotiating deals to do them, and monitoring to ensure they are successful. Some of these could be large and high profile, such as one or more 'Olympic reserves', for example in tropical forests, to be managed long term to offset the Games' greenhouse gas emissions.

A 'sustainability implant'?
This work could potentially provide a 'banquet for consultants'. It would probably be carried out better, more persuasively and much more cheaply through some kind of agency embedded in the main Olympics project management structure in order to work very closely with it, but responsible for promoting the environmental agenda, and with independent reporting lines and accountability. This closely integrated but semi-independent function might be analogous to Internal Audit or a travel agent 'implant' in a corporation, so we suggest the

term 'sustainability implant'. It would need to report to some external steering group. This could involve some combination of the national environmental agencies, the Sustainable Development Commission and NGOs with sustainability interests.

Strategic Environmental Assessment and project level Environmental Impact Assessment should be very helpful. However another management tool, Quality of Life Assessment, developed by the Countryside Agency, Environment Agency, English Nature and English Heritage, may be even more useful because it revolves around the idea of substitution of benefits as set out in this chapter, and offers a systematic process for applying it.

Changing perceptions and habits

Two of the main barriers to sustainable behaviour change are image – green options are often perceived as inferior, un-cool, even faintly absurd – and habit – people do not keep making careful conscious decisions about their day-to-day travel, consumption, routine, but tend to carry on doing what they have always done and save their cognitive energy for other things. One of the biggest challenges facing sustainable consumption initiatives is to break the inertia: get people to re-evaluate their perceptions and routines anew.

The Olympics offer a wonderful opportunity for doing so because they are a huge special occasion, which will take all participants out of their normal routines briefly but intensely. The barrier of habit and inertia will already be broken. If they see and experience sustainability in action in the buildings, planning, movement, infrastructure and consumption during the Olympics, they may well carry the change back into normal life.

Some of the environmental initiatives proposed here offer opportunities for spectacle and pageantry that could add to the Games' aura while conveying important messages. For example, tens of thousands of cyclists cruising across London between different Olympic venues in much less time and effort than would otherwise be needed might not only show the role cycling can play in urban utility travel in the UK, but perhaps prompt the Chinese

Government to see its mass cycling as an asset to be exploited rather than a shameful hangover from the past. The spectacle of national delegations arriving in their own trains from remote and exotic places could kick start a revival of long distance rail travel as both practical and romantic.

The Olympics as a force for global (environmental) peace and progress?

Warring Greek city states all observed an Olympic truce to allow athletes to travel safely to the Olympic Games and compete peaceably. Once everybody was safely home afterwards the wars started up again. The modern Games aspire to the same ideal of sporting competition acting as a force for peace. They have not managed to secure a global truce, perhaps partly because this is no longer necessary to allow participants to travel safely to the Games (though perhaps the proposal to encourage national delegations to come by transcontinental train could be a catalyst for reopening some frontiers).

However an environmental reinterpretation of the idea would be to call on all participating countries to suspend their hostilities against the planet – that is, refrain from damaging the environment for the twenty nine days of the Games – and perhaps a few days either side. Of course it would impossible for all the world's power stations, air services and cars to stop for around three weeks. However twenty nine days is just under eight per cent of the year. An invitation for all participating nations to mark the Games with action to reduce their environmental damage and resource depletion by seven per cent or eight per cent spread over the year would achieve a similar result as a four week 'environment truce' but with the merit of being practicable and achievable without inordinate pain or disruption.

The Olympic link and the 'one-off' nature of the proposal might make this politically attractive, or at least palatable, to countries which have resisted commitments from other sources. The most alarming current 'rogue state' is the USA, whose refusal to support global initiatives to reduce greenhouse gas emissions has been rated by sober scientific observers as a greater threat to peace and security than any terrorism or weapons of mass destruction. Hopefully this position will have changed by 2012 but there will doubtless be other blockages in global environmental diplomacy which an appeal to the Olympic spirit might help resolve.

Conclusion

The seemingly impossible goal of holding the Olympics with not only 'no negative net impact on the environment' but also 'a positive green legacy' is within London's reach. To achieve this, the principle of minimising impacts then substituting any remaining ones needs to be embedded in the planning, management and decision processes of the Olympics.

This will require a more proactive, interventionist, public interest-driven delivery process than has been politically fashionable in the UK for some time. But this will be needed anyway to ensure – and reassure the IOC – that London will deliver everything needed successfully and on time.

The positive green legacy could extend well beyond London to include long term shifts in attitudes and behaviour towards more sustainable approaches, reinvigorating alternatives to air travel, and even launching an international programme of impact reduction.

None of this would detract from or compete with the Olympic's central sporting purpose. On the contrary: it would enhance participants' experience of the Games, help reduce the risks inherent in such an event, and reinvigorate the Game's historic role promoting peace and cooperation between nations.

5 Stuck in the Blocks? A sustainable sporting legacy

Fred Coalter

5 Stuck in the Blocks?
A sustainable sporting legacy
Fred Coalter

As part of the promotional materials for the London 2012 Olympic Bid the claim is made that, if the Bid is successful:

> grassroots participation would be boosted. An already sports-mad nation would get fitter and healthier.

In other words, the staging of the Olympic Games in London would lead to 'a step change in the nation's physical activity', contributing to the Government's desire to increase participation in sport and physical activity. Such claims suggest that holding the Olympic Games in London can contribute to the Government's broader social and health agenda. It is also claimed that it will contribute to the extremely ambitious target of seventy per cent of the population undertaking 5x30 minutes of moderate activity per week by 2020 as outlined in *Game Plan* (DCMS/Cabinet Office 2002), the Government's strategy for delivering its sport and physical activity objectives.

However, the model of behaviour change underpinning such claims is not clear. Is it implying a media-led growth in participation as a result of widespread coverage of the Olympic Bid? Is it presuming that elite sporting role models will encourage widespread participation? Is it assuming that the coverage of individual sports will increase their popularity (even though many Olympic sports are highly technical and/or minority activities)? Why is it assuming that persistently under-participating groups will be moved to participate and enable the nation to get fitter and healthier? As the great majority of spectators of any Olympics will view it via television, what is specific about a London Games? Will any of the presumed impacts be restricted to the South East of England, where provision and a sense of involvement will be concentrated?

This chapter addresses some of these questions and examines the extent to which any successful London Bid might leave a 'sporting participation heritage' (rather than simply a facility heritage). It will examine the following issues:

- The scale of the challenge to increase sports participation and existing evidence about the contribution of large scale sports events.

- The opportunities and challenges implied by the use of sporting role models and the development of sports volunteering.

- Some conclusions about the need to 'embed' the Olympics in a broader strategy for sports development.

The Scale of the Challenge

The ambitious nature of the Game Plan (DCMS/Cabinet Office 2002) target is indicated by the fact that it will require an increase of more than one hundred per cent on the current levels of participation – only thirty per cent of the population currently meet the Government's target for health-related physical activity levels (Sport England 2004). Although the Game Plan target is not based simply on sports participation, but on wider aspects of physical activity, the contribution of sport will require a sea change in current trends. An increase in sports participation in the 1980s has been followed by relative stagnation in the 1990s. Figure 5.1 illustrates both stagnation and stubbornly persistent class-based differences.

Figure 5.2 illustrates that, despite recent increases in participation among older age groups, there is still a strong relationship between age and sports participation.

Further, despite increases in the late 1980s and early 1990s, women's overall participation remains less than men's and concentrated in a much narrower band of activities. Further, cultural shifts

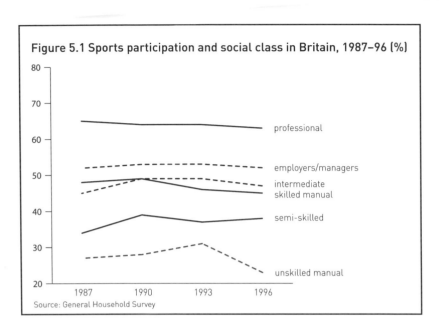

Figure 5.1 Sports participation and social class in Britain, 1987–96 (%)

professional
employers/managers
intermediate
skilled manual
semi-skilled
unskilled manual

Source: General Household Survey

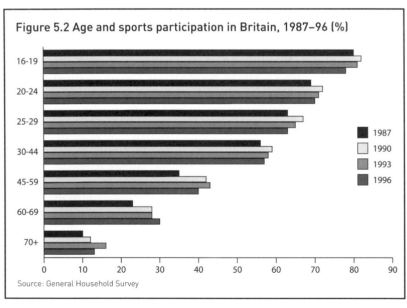

Figure 5.2 Age and sports participation in Britain, 1987–96 (%)

1987
1990
1993
1996

Source: General Household Survey

and increased pressure on time has led to a shift away from traditional, Olympic-type, sports to forms of activity which are flexible, individualistic and non-competitive (e.g. aerobics, hi-tech fitness, cycling, walking) (Coalter 1999).

Such long-term stagnation and changing trends in sports participation pose major challenges, both for general attempts to increase sports participation and, more directly, for the claimed contribution of the Olympic Games.

Impact of events on general sports participation: survey evidence
Despite the substantial claims made about the wider social impacts of major sporting events, there is a lack of rigorous post-games evaluation (Cashman 2003). More specifically, in relation to our concerns, there is little research on the impact of major events on sports development (Hindson et al 1994). Nevertheless, the data that do exist are sufficient to raise critical questions about some of the assumptions underpinning the London 2012 claims about its potential impact on sports participation, although some also provide an indication as to how to maximise the impact of an event on sports participation.

There is very little participation data permitting an evaluation of the impact of the Olympics on general levels of sports participation. However, Veal (2003), in an analysis of sports participation in Australia between 1985 and 2002, provides some indicative data. Although the analysis is concerned with methodological issues that limit longitudinal analysis, Veal does provide comparable data for 2000/1 and 2001/2, before and after the Sydney Olympics.

In the year following the 2000 Games, although seven Olympic sports experienced a small increase in participation, nine declined. The pattern for non-Olympic sports was broadly similar, with the biggest increase in non-competitive walking. Veal (2003) also speculates that declines in participation for certain sports could be explained by a 'couch potato' syndrome induced by so much sports coverage on television! However, his overall conclusion is that it is 'a mixed picture . . . difficult to attribute it to the Olympic Games'.

UK Sport commissioned research on the 2002 Manchester Commonwealth Games indicates broadly similar results (MORI, 2004). Although survey results show that respondents felt that the Games had had a positive effect on their playing and watching habits, overall sports participation and membership of sports clubs in Greater Manchester declined in the post-Games period. As the measured 'declines' were within the usual margin of error for survey data, we can simply conclude that the Commonwealth Games made no measurable impact on immediate post-Games participation.

A recent report on the impact of the highly publicised curling Olympic gold medal on participation in curling in Scotland (**sport**scotland, 2004) concluded that:

> the success has had the greatest impact on those who were already active in sport. Consequently, care should be taken when asserting that success on the world stage in sport has an impact on general levels of participation.

Such an analysis is also supported by *Game Plan* (DCMS/Cabinet Office 2002), which concluded that 'it would seem that hosting events is not an effective, value for money, method of achieving . . . a sustained increase in mass participation'.

On the basis of the data presented above it is clear that the London 2012 Bid needs to be careful about how it presents the potential 'Olympic effect', avoiding raising expectations which it cannot fulfil and possibly alienating support within the wider sporting community. A key issue here will be addressing the concerns, whether valid or not, about Lottery funding being diverted away from community sports development to support the London 2012 Bid.

More generally, given the clear difficulties in isolating any 'Olympic effect', it would seem inappropriate to establish strategic sports participation targets related directly to a successful Olympics. However, it may be possible to propose targets for increased participation rates at sporting facilities in the Lower Lea Valley. Another possible approach might be to move beyond the broad aggregate targets used under the Government's Public Service Agreement approach, towards incremental targets for individual sports, especially those involved directly in Olympic competition.

Clearly, if a London 2012 Games is to make any contribution to a sustained increase in sports participation, it must be as a partner in a much broader development strategy, with a wide range of organisations seeking to build on the heightened profile of sport. This chapter will now turn to some of these issues.

Impact on participation: governing bodies and clubs

Although there are good reasons to understand the lack of measurable impact of major games on general participation, it might be expected that they would have more impact on sports clubs, especially those for Olympic sports. Again, very little evaluation of this hypothesis has been undertaken. However, one study undertaken in New Zealand (Hindson *et al* 1994), provides a rather pessimistic analysis (especially if reliance is placed solely on some presumed 'trickle down effect').

The analysis is based on a postal survey of 35 New Zealand sports clubs and six National Sporting Organisations (NSOs) in the period following the 1992 Albertville Winter Olympics and Barcelona Olympics Games. The purpose of the survey was to examine the impact of these events on club membership. The evidence for a 'trickle down effect' was very limited, with only six of the clubs having an increase in membership enquiries. Only three experienced an increase in competitive membership, with two increasing 'social' (i.e. recreational) membership.

However, Hindson *et al* (1994) do not simply conclude that the Winter and Summer Games had no effect on sporting demand. They also point to a series of supply-side failures, in which both the NSOs and clubs failed to capitalise on the publicity surrounding the Games. For example, they conclude that there was:

■ A lack of innovative marketing. Only four clubs used the Games as a marketing and promotion tool.

- A general failure to forward plan and to market and promote the sport in the run up to the games.

- Both NSOs and sports clubs were simply complacent, relying on an anticipated 'trickle down effect' from Olympic coverage to promote sport.

- The relationship between NSOs and clubs was not conducive to capitalising on the promotional opportunities provided by the Games, with the NSOs being wholly concerned with competitive sport and having little interest in the recreational ('social') sporting activities of clubs. As a consequence, opportunities to promote the various sports in a coherent national strategy were lost.

As the authors conclude: 'trickle down benefits from the Olympics are not automatic'. (Hindson *et al* 1994). Unless the Games are embedded in a longer-term developmental strategy they are very unlikely to have any general, and only limited sports-specific, impacts (this point will be returned to later).

These concerns prompt issues about the roles and responsibilities of governing bodies and sports clubs in capitalising on the 'Olympic effect'. Some issues for consideration are:

- The need for an influential 'sports legacy champion' within the London 2012 organisation. This would ensure that sports legacy issues are sufficiently considered and that liaison with all relevant organisations (including the relevant local authorities) was central to the Bid. This post should act as a catalyst to promote a more holistic approach to planning for sports development, both before and after the Olympic Games.

- Regional sports boards and national sporting bodies must be encouraged and supported to maximise on the publicity and profile associated with the Games.

- Governing bodies of sport, especially Olympic sports, should be given specific participation targets during this pre-Olympic period. As part of this, governing bodies need to engage more effectively at local level.

Opportunities and challenges

Sporting role models and mass participation

However, in addition to concerns about supply-side failures Hindson *et al* (1994) raise a further, fundamental, issue. They question the extent to which the competitive excellence associated with Olympic Games could be effective in promoting recreational sport at a local level. In opposition to the 'role model' thesis, in which people are inspired to emulate the feats of sporting heroes, the authors suggest that it is equally possible that sporting and technical excellence can reduce non-participants' feelings of self-efficacy, leading them to conclude that they do not have the necessary skills and competence to participate in sport. As Hindson *et al* (1994) conclude:

> sports organisations need to ensure that marketing is sensitive to consumer resistance arising from an awareness of how difficult it is . . . to emulate our sporting heroes and heroines.

This reflects a more general questioning of the nature of any presumed link between sporting excellence and mass participation (DCMS/Cabinet Office, 2002). In this regard it is possible to suggest that there are several, increasingly unconnected, 'worlds of sport':

■ Sporting events/spectacle (driven by economic and political imperatives).

■ Sporting excellence (driven by talent identification and specialist sports science support and, in some cases, banned drugs).

■ Recreational sport and clubs (driven by competition, enjoyment of sport and sociability and local authority investment in facilities)

■ Social inclusion, government-driven policies which attempt to use sport for instrumental purposes (e.g. crime reduction; health improvement) that are more likely to be provided by youth workers or health professionals than coaches.

Further, Payne *et al* (2003) in a wide-ranging review of literature, illustrate that much thinking about the relationship between sporting role models and wider sports participation fails to understand the complexity of processes of learning and behavioural change. They illustrate that role model programmes (RMPs) form a continuum: from a single exposure event (role model visit to school/club) to approaches based on long term mentoring and systematic reinforcement – with success in changing attitudes and behaviour related to the length and intensity of contact with any role models. The review illustrates a number of factors of direct relevance to the sporting role model approach, which seems to be implicit in the London 2012 claims.

Firstly, the target audience needs to perceive that the role model is both relevant and accessible. Relevance relates to a number of factors, including race and gender – the review highlights data that suggest that there are important gender differences in the perception of relevant role models. Young males are much more likely than females to view sports people as role models, although some might argue that this is because of a lack of female sporting role models in the media. Secondly, the extent to which individuals adopt role models relates to personal perceptions of self-efficacy and outcome expectancy – the extent to which individuals perceive that they can achieve acceptable levels of performance and obtain positive outcomes. Learning is more likely to occur when the learner perceives that they are capable of carrying out the behaviour and thinks that there is a high probability that the behaviour will result in a particular, desirable, outcome.

This reflects Hindson *et al*'s (1994) suggestion that sporting excellence might not be the most appropriate role model for achieving increased recreational participation and getting the nation 'fitter and healthier'. Payne *et al*'s (2003) third concern about role models is an increasingly widespread one – sporting role models are not always positive. Many aspects of professional sport (violence, cheating, disputing decisions, feigning injury, drugs) fall short of the Olympic ideal.

Where these issues can be addressed, Payne *et al* (1994) suggest that, to be successful, any role model programme must have the following elements:

■ *Provision of ongoing, needs-oriented, support for participants:* Programmes need to take account of the needs and competencies of the target audience, with attention given to the selection and training of mentors and on-going support.

■ *Ongoing reminders of role models' message:* The nature of the positive attitudes and behaviours need to be reinforced constantly

■ *Support and encouragement of a variety of role models:* Sporting role models need to be supported and embedded in a wider support network in including the involvement of parents, teachers and significant adults.

The overall conclusion is that sporting role model programmes need to be 'embedded' – part of a more general, on-going, programme of support. Fleeting media images of sporting achievement may not be enough to ensure that such role models contribute to a substantial increase in sports participation. There is a need for a more systematic and integrated approach which links the promotion of national sporting heroes to support for local role models, who can develop on-going relationships with local people and communities.

Volunteering in sport

Volunteering is an aspect of major events that has the potential to contribute to social regeneration and the strengthening of social capital (although its effects are likely to be geographically limited). A study of the 2002 Manchester Commonwealth Games (ICRCTHI 2003) found that 23,000 people applied to be volunteers, with 9,000 being selected. Of those selected, a quarter (twenty four per cent) had no previous volunteering experience and over half (fifty three per cent) were under the age of forty five. While older volunteers were motivated by wanting to 'give something back', young ones were more instrumental, being motivated by a desire for personal and skill development.

However, while it is clear that volunteering provided a fulfilling and productive experience for those chosen, its broader impact on increasing sports participation may have been rather limited. For example, ninety two per cent of the volunteers claimed to have taken part in sport or physical activity in the previous twelve months, eighty seven per cent on a 'regular basis' – participation levels far above the national average (e.g. in 1966 the General Household Survey indicated that only thirty two per cent of the adult population had taken part in sport in the previous four weeks) – and only four per cent said that they had no interest in sport. Consequently, although this may also reflect the nature of the selection procedures, this seems a case of preaching to the converted and may have had limited impact on sports development.

Further, the volunteering programme appears to have been very limited in terms of inclusivity, with ninety two per cent of volunteers being white British. Ritchie (2000) also refers to this issue in an evaluation of the Calgary Olympics. Ritchie suggests that as volunteerism has the potential to make a substantial contribution to civic pride and social cohesion, although there is a need to adopt formal procedures for the registration and recognition of volunteer efforts. Further, because of the multi-cultural nature of large-scale events, efforts need to be made to recruit more volunteers from ethnic minorities (who can also contribute to the multi-lingual and multi-cultural nature of such events). Waitt (2001) also addresses the issue of the relationship of minority ethnic groups to such celebratory events. Via a survey of Sydney residents prior to the 2000 Olympics, Waitt (2001) concluded that theories of 'civic boosterism' were supported. Overall, two years before the Olympics, respondents had positive feelings of national achievement, civic pride and community spirit as a result of the prospect of hosting the Games. The interesting fact for Waitt (2001) was that the most enthusiastic were under fifty and non-English speaking. Waitt (2001) concludes that:

> Those most enthusiastic about the games are perhaps exactly the people amongst whom the Federal and State Governments would wish to engender feelings of belonging to the 'imagined community' of Australia and a greater community through the identification of self and place.

Available literature on volunteering in major games indicates the substantial potential to use such events as a catalyst for community and multi-cultural involvement. However, in terms of widening participation in sport, the Manchester experience indicates that such events may only attract those already committed to sport.

Interestingly, Cashman (2003) implies that if the catalytic impact of games for the host community is to be sustained, there is a need to plan for what happens after them, to provide some degree of continuity (see also Ritchie 2000). Cashman (2003) argues that there is a need to:

> plan for the immediate post-games period when there is often a great sense of loss experienced by many members of the host community, even a post-games depression.

This argument for the need for post-games planning raises a more general point about viewing such events as being only one part of a much longer and systematic process of both sporting and community development.

Meeting the Challenge

Embedding the Olympics: the need for a strategy

We have already noted Hindson *et al*'s (1994) comments about the dangers in depending on a 'trickle-down effect' and the need for systematic promotion of sport in the period running up to major games. Further, Payne *et al* (2003) also argue that sporting role models need to be embedded in systematic programmes of development. This need to 'embed' a Games in broader processes of development is also supported by Ritchie (2000). Reflecting on the Calgary Winter Olympics Ritchie (2000) makes four strategic points:

- Legacy planning needs to ensure that the enthusiasm for the 'event window' is maintained by ensuring that sporting commitments are consolidated prior to event to ensure post-event commitment.

- There is a need for annual sporting events ('mini games'), before and after the main event.

- The Olympic facilities must be available to public, before and after the event.

- There is need to adopt a 'community development' approach, by understanding and building on the values of local residents and stakeholders.

There is some indication that elements of this approach have been adopted by the London 2012 Bid. For example, following the model adopted for the Manchester Commonwealth Games, the majority of the proposed capital investment is based on a strategic evaluation of the longer-term sports development needs of the South East (if not the particular local authorities who will host the games and be responsible for subsequent revenue and maintenance). Further, Roger Draper (2003:16), the Chief Executive of Sport England, has commented that:

> We are totally in support of the Olympics, but what we have said is that it has to leave a legacy. It's got to be twin tracked. It's no good having a great Olympics in 2012 and inspiring many young people to take up sport if we don't have the facilities, coaching and infrastructure to get them involved and keep them in sport.

Most of the evidence quoted here suggests that major sporting events have no inevitably positive impacts on levels of sports participation. Further, many of the implicit assumptions about stimulating participation (sporting role models, 'trickle down effects', media coverage) are at best simplistic as single variable theories of behavioural change. While events such as the Olympic Games may have some role to play, this is only as part of a much more systematic and strategic developmental approach. This appears to be partly recognised by London 2012, who state that the physical infrastructure of the Games needs to be supported by:

- sustained government investment;

- local authority commitment to sport;

- re-establishing sport in schools;

- developing grass roots coaching programmes;

- commitment of Department of Health to sport and physical activity.

In fact, without being too cynical, one might conclude that, if this is done, in terms of sports development, there is little need for the Olympics! One of the most significant challenges would be, therefore, to ensure that a London 2012 Olympic Games acts as a catalyst in bringing these programmes forward.

In this regard a comment about the Lottery Sports Fund seems relevant. There has been some concern about the extent to which London 2012 could divert Lottery funding from community sports development. With the various reservations about the 'Olympic effect', there may be a case for arguing that an increase in sports participation would be more likely to be achieved via direct, local, investment. Because some aspects of facility planning for London 2012 are based on the sporting needs of the South East of England, investment is not based wholly on the 'diversion' of Lottery funding from sports development. However, it is clear that if the London 2012 Bid is successful, additional money will need to be diverted from broader investments in sport. For example, a front page headline in the Scotsman of 9 January 2004 proclaimed: '**Olympics setback for sport in Scotland** London bid may cost sport in Scotland £40m'.

In the accompanying article an unnamed spokesperson for **sport**scotland was quoted as saying:

> There is a terrible irony in the fact that bringing the greatest sporting show on earth to the UK could devastate the regeneration of sport in Scotland and set us back 20 years.

While this may seem a rather apocalyptic analysis, it does express widespread concern within sport that the proclaimed aims of boosting grassroots participation and achieving a fitter and healthier nation might be better achieved by more direct investment in sporting infrastructure. For example, a recent unpublished **sport**england report, *The Condition and Refurbishment of Public Sector Sports Facilities*, concluded that, to sustain the current level of public sports halls and swimming pools, there was a need for £110 million extra expenditure per year for five years. One conclusion from this might be that, even if the Olympics led to an increase in sports participation, the physical infrastructure for sport may not be able to cater for such demand. Taken together, these issues present some obvious challenges for investment in sport. Some options for consideration are:

- Both HM Treasury and DfES should be approached to obtain funding to improve grassroots sports participation. The London 2012 and heightened government interest in sport provides an unprecedented opportunity to make this case. Expenditure of the Olympic Bid should not be instead of continued investment in grass-roots sport.

- A Sport Endowment Fund could be set up with donations from visitors to the Olympic site and corporate sources.

- At a more local level, the London boroughs within which it is proposed to hold the Games, would argue strongly that the emphasis must be on local-led regeneration and that the issue of subsequent revenue costs for the facilities in the Olympic Village must be addressed. One potential option here may be the establishment of a trust to ensure that any profits are reinvested into maintaining the facilities.

Conclusion

As suggested in *Game Plan* (DCMS/Cabinet Office 2002), celebration, economic regeneration, tourism development, international prestige and spectacle may be legitimate reasons for public investment in an Olympic Games. However, existing evidence suggests that the presumed 'trickle-down effects' of general increases in sports participation and a general improvement in fitness and health are unlikely direct outcomes of a successful Olympic Games Bid. Leaving aside the not inconsiderable problem that sporting excellence may not be the best model for encouraging 'grassroots participation', in terms of broader strategic outcomes the Olympic Games can only be regarded as only one element in a much broader, long-term, developmental programme.

If large-scale changes in sports participation are to occur, this will be the result of complex (and not well understood) interactions between such factors as changing public attitudes and values, changing distributions of work time, sustained government investment in schools and improved infrastructure of quality local facilities. Within this broader social strategy, the Bid for the 2012 Olympic Games may act as a catalyst for some forms of sports participation, if some of the following steps are taken:

■ Governing bodies and clubs need to work together more closely to develop innovative marketing and promotional campaigns that capitalise on the high profile media coverage of the London 2012 Bid.

■ The Bid for the Olympic Games should be viewed as only one part in a broader process, with a programme of pre- and post-Games inclusive events throughout the country.

■ The relevance of sporting role models and associated images of excellence need to be carefully considered. Where such models are used, they need to be embedded in systematic and ongoing local programmes of promotion, mentoring and support.

■ The potential of Olympic volunteering programmes to develop commitment beyond the Olympics and the potential sustainable contribution to the sporting infrastructure needs careful planning.

■ If the Bid for the 2012 Olympic Games is taken as an indicator of a renewed government commitment to sport, a failed bid should not be used as a reason for reduced public investment in sport. To fail to build on the greatly increased profile for sport could be regarded as a rather cynical use of sport for non-sporting purposes.

6 Just Another Ceremony? A sustainable cultural legacy

Keith Khan

6 Just Another Ceremony?
A sustainable cultural legacy
Keith Khan

When the first reveller bedecked in feathers and finery jumped up in the grey and narrow streets of Notting Hill in 1964, it was a creative and a subversive act. That reveller was against the wind, the street and the establishment. Forty years on in 2004 that same reveller is merely a puppet of the local government, the police, manipulated by the state. The culture of carnival has become a feud of the under-funded, resulting in the lack of respect and status that these artists have. Above all else, that same reveller is now a fossil – an artefact, and someone dislocated against the current climate; that costume a snapshot of the past, seen against the sound systems, DJ's and black British style.

Culture and creativity are inherently disruptive. They pose a threat to systems of authority but are also the lifeblood of healthy liberal societies. Rooted in individual interpretation and connected to the past, they shun the definition of grand narratives and wrong-foot those who attempt to control them. In order for London to stage a successful Olympics in 2012, it will have to actively engage these unpredictable forces as a means to bring relevance and ownership to the Games for the people of London, throughout the UK and the wider world.

But this is just the beginning of the challenge. Past experience shows that the problematic for Olympic cultural planners is complex: something that would hardly be eased were the Games to be held in London. Those charged with designing a four-year cultural programme and overseeing the display of culture during the Games will have to:

- Represent a spectrum of cultural activity yet also convey a common sense of national identity.

- Reconcile the values of Olympian internationalism with those national and civic distinctiveness.

- Achieve this in Britain, a country sensitive to any debates surrounding culture and identity.

As a response to this challenge this chapter outlines:

- the purpose of culture;

- a framework of guidelines for cultural initiatives;

- some hypothetical ideas for cultural programming.

The function of culture in the Olympics should be to develop understanding. This applies both on the inside in the areas directly affected by the Olympics and on the outside, in the eyes of those who will watch those places. In this way culture in the Olympics should be used to discover, celebrate and understand one's own cultural identity, but also understand that which belongs to others.

Discovering cultural identity

The Olympics is an opportunity to reappraise what it is to live in the UK, in London and in the East End of London. Rather than telling the story of Britain through past hegemonies and institutions we can use the cultural programme to engage the nation in a process of cultural discovery. Nowhere is this more important than in the East End, an area that has had its cultural heritage buried in the official discourse and caricatured in the popular one.

Perception influence

While there is a need to inwardly discover and learn, if the cultural programme is carefully devised it can form the basis for a constructive impression of Britain to be conveyed throughout the world. This is not simply about Britain, but London too. While the East End has a shady image, the Thames Gateway's is positively negative. The Olympic Bid represents not just a catalyst to physical regeneration, but a chance to change the way the region is viewed through the active use and display of culture and creativity.

The success of these objectives is mutually intertwined; they have to complement rather than contradict one another. We will fail if we try and manufacture something with a hollow sense of homogeneity or nationalism. Instead, we have to be robust and daring, and create something without precedent. Crucially if the use of culture is to have integrity and not be prone to inconsistencies and contradictions it must be used to investigate questions rather than display answers.

Taking such an approach to culture is intended to assist the staging of successful Games. But in focusing upon the needs and aspirations of people the proposals are as much to do with the role of art and culture in enriching urban renewal and wider society as they are to do with staging an Olympics.

A rich cultural past and vibrant creative present are not the stuff of mere whim. They reflect London, are of socio-economic importance and in terms of staging a successful Games, a principal national asset. Current proposals concerning the role of culture, draw attention to this, but ultimately sell Britain short. This relates to a lack of understanding of the position of culture and a wariness of stepping away from the comfort zone of London's historically renowned museums and galleries. The difficulty and lack of understanding surrounding its role need not be seen as an obstacle, but as a liberating opportunity to stage a sustainable, culturally vibrant and creative Games. The first step towards this is an appreciation of the problems surrounding 'culture'.

The cultural challenge

I come, as most Londoners do from a culturally schizophrenic background. I am able to sift through multiple identities – from popular to polyglottal. To me the term 'culture' essentially refers to two separate but related concepts.

It can be used as a term to refer to a way of life specific to a certain group of individuals. For example, in such a context, people might speak of 'the British culture'. In this sense 'culture' is used as a byword for identity. Culture can also be used as a term to refer to creative expressions; the products and action of cultural activity. Culture in this context could be used to refer to the contents of The National Gallery, the catch all 'Bollywood', Verdi's *Requiem* or perhaps *The Simpsons*.

While the term 'culture' concerns the related concepts of identity and activity, in the context of nation states, the two understandings are not necessarily complementary. With the contemporary prominence of highly individualized multi-faceted identities and a society that permits their display, it is hard for populations to collectively subscribe to cultural activity that they feel explains national cultural identity.

The planning of the 2012 Olympics however, demands that both interpretations of culture have to be represented. This is the challenge for cultural planners and is by no means a simple task, when applied to Britain.

Britain vs the UK

In terms of a nation struggling with notions of national identity in the context of complex individual identities, we are a case in point. Over the past fifty years Britain has been in a process of transition. The decline of deference, shared values, institutions and faith in the political process have been accompanied by a reluctance to feel at ease with a singular, national 'cultural identity'. Many of our recognised national symbols (The Union Jack – we have redrawn it, re-coloured it and even reclaimed it) feel like little more than a hangover of a bygone era; with no connection to the reality of living in Britain today. It is no longer possible to explain what it is to be British in a series of buildings, literature and painting. Even the words 'British' and 'Britain' seem somewhat negatively loaded. The UK infact, as a opposed to 'Britain' increasingly appears as the proper noun of choice in pop culture: UK Garage, CDUK, UK Gold and FCUK.

While there is a current unease at referring to British cultural identity, Britain is undeniably rich in cultural activity:

- Britain leads the world with its creative industries sector, with leading lights emerging in the field of new technology, design and the built environment.

- Britain is unique in identifying links between education, industry and creativity.

- The museum sector can promote an imaginative understanding of history, science and the arts, linking the past to the present.

- Within the performing arts, there is a seemingly endless resource of writing, cutting edge and performing talent.

- The music industry is creating fascinating and imaginative links between established and emerging talent.

- Britain is renowned for its 'techno local' film making facilities – with both Indian and American industries using these resources extensively.

- The arts sector is re-interpreting its vision, and creating a visionary pool of ideas about process and talent.

These are by no means fully representative, but give some indications of the breadth of UK culture. Much of the ambiguity surrounding what it means to be British is both a reflection of and caused by this cultural richness. So while London and Britain have no common cultural identity in immediately obvious symbols, habits and ways of life; this is counterweighted by vibrant diversity and cultural activity.

Cultural planners in Britain have had to address these tensions, to varying degrees of success, in two major non-sporting events.

The Millennium Dome, 2000
This project (like the Forum in Barcelona), has become memorable for the building itself – an amazing piece of tensile engineering, rather than its content. This was flawed as it aimed to provide a complex

message for all. Ultimately, it became too non-specific and didactic to reach a mass audience. The building was designed to be temporary, while the impact of its content was hoped to have a permanent legacy. I worked with the creative team of Mark Fisher and Peter Gabriel – and luckily we were given artistic autonomy – leading to a central show that was individualistic, eclectic and eccentric. Other segments were blighted by 'committee workin'. Investment in ideas and individuals with clear vision works.

Queen's Golden Jubilee, 2002
The Commonwealth parade was deemed a success because it was a challenge to how Britain looked and felt. The Royal Family and the Palace were happy to engage with a risky rewriting of the ceremonial and the participatory. Much of this played with out blurred identities and sense of dual nationality – London as a world city, containing fragments of the world. It was fascinating for me to work with many disenfranchised communities and engage with other views of culture and arts. Of the four thousand people in the parade, only three hundred (Akademi and Adzdido) came from the arts council's stable of artists and cultural practice. It displayed the inability of our current arts funding system to deal with diversity, if the practice of the artist is not recognized as 'high' or even acceptable culture. At motiroti, along with Ali Zaidi, we created an international schools project with the participation of children from the seventy two Commonwealth countries. Their input was transformed (they made over two thousand drawings and messages) into a triumphal arch way through which the queen could process. Thus, we tied education and national splendour into one event.

The Olympic Paradox

The official values of the Olympic movement are Sport, Education and Culture. Despite culture being placed on an equal footing with sport in the Olympic Movement, in some senses culture and the Olympics resemble an unholy alliance. Fundamentally sporting excellence is something that can be measured in objective terms, while artistic and creative excellence can only be measured in subjective terms. The London Olympics of 1948 were the last to award medals alongside the Games for artistic achievement. With their passing went the artificial attempt to judge sport and culture on the same terms. Culture is thus shrouded in tension in Olympic Games planning as it introduces subjective notions of excellence to a theatre that is traditionally intended to be impartial, neutral and objective.

The ancient Olympics originally represented a break for the warring factions of Ancient Greece to compete at sport in an environment cleansed of difference and identity; a means to escape cultural difference. Although the modern Olympics are imbued with the universal ideology of internationalism, humanity and truce, the pressure to convey national distinctiveness and civic culture have the capacity to emphasise difference rather than neutralise it.

Within the modern Olympic Games, this has resulted in an accepted segeway of culture and sport. Packaging, symbolic messaging and 'entertainment' have become the role of cultural segments, something that has come to manifest itself in the iconography of the Games.

In terms of the ceremonial, torch-bearing has become the ultimate expression of Olympic cultural idealism in the context of the host nation. An emphasis has been bought to bear on this person to encapsulate the dimensions of a nation's multiple identities. At Atlanta in 1996, Muhammad Ali caressed America's race nerve, representing harmony between black and white, able and disabled, while embodying the ideals of courage, determination and athleticism. Cathy Freeman in 2000 represented the similar reconciliation between aboriginal and white in Australia while symbolising equality between the sexes and technological endeavour in her hi-tech tracksuit. Antonio Rebello, the disabled archer who lit the torch at Barcelona in 1992 symbolised elements of all of the above while illustrating the rediscovered beauty of the Olympic city.

But iconography can only go so far. In many ways it becomes a substitute for a genuine reconciliation of the challenge to our notions of culture posed by the Olympics. This has often resulted in a disjuncture between the high ideals represented in iconography and the real experience of people's engagement with culture. While Muhammad Ali may have represented the unity of black and white, the Games still took place in a divided city, with the poor, mostly black population living to the south and the rich mostly white population living to the north.

The rise in the importance of a four year series of cultural events, the 'Olympic Cultural Programme' has aimed to fill this gap. Sydney 2000 showed that a cultural programme can still leave people feeling short-changed. Ceremonies pitched the country as fun, contemporary, beach loving, but crucially within the socio-political context of the 'the spirit of reconciliation' between Australia's races. The aboriginal segment, however, created a fixed sense of identity in the world's eye for aboriginal people as earthy, raw and potentially played into the idea that diversity means exoticising rather than accepting difference. Alongside this, Sydney's cultural programme failed to dovetail into the Games:

> At the time of the sporting competitions, all arts performances were concentrated in the Sydney opera house at elevated prices, with an emphasis on European high art . . . The final festival programme lacked ethnic diversity and geographical spread, even within the host city. Accordingly it was criticised for being elitist and inaccessible to the general public (Frankland 2000).

The uses of cultural programming

So, how to respond to the challenge? Past experience shows that it is difficult to synthesise the complexity of modern society without contradictions emerging. Although the development of a cultural programme has deepened the potential of culture to have an impact upon lives. The way in which it is used and the ends to which it is deployed will determine how sustained its impact is. In light of this, it is essential to interrogate what culture is actually good for.

At its heart, culture is an aid to understanding, both an understanding of one's own culture and values and those of others. It was this that underpinned the Cultural Programming surrounding the Manchester Commonwealth Games of 2002, as part of which an innovative education programme engaged 75,000 primary school children in 750 events linking children with countries throughout the Commonwealth.

In the context of the London Olympics, culture provides a similar opportunity to provoke the discovery and expression of personal cultural identity. While secondly, in the context of an international mega-event it can influence the way an area of Britain is understood at home and how the nation itself is perceived overseas.

Discovery of personal cultural identity

The United Nations' Universal Declaration of Human Rights of 1948, Article 27 (1) enshrines this commitment to the rights of everybody to have access to and enjoy the fruits of human culture:

> Everyone has the right freely to participate in the cultural life of the community, to enjoy the arts, and to share in scientific advancement and its benefits.

In the years that have followed, these sentiments have echoed in policy documents and ministerial statements. DCMS's *Culture and Creativity: the next ten years*, devoted a chapter to 'widening participation and access' (2001). The Olympic Bid represents an unprecedented opportunity to realise some of these ideals.

I believe that Londoners are hoping for a cultural programme in which they see themselves reflected. It provides London with the opportunity to discover the heritage of people who have lived and live in the city, rather than perpetuating the stories of the institutions and powerful elites, popularly associated with the capital. Nowhere is this more important than in the area directly effected by the Bid. For centuries the East End has been a refuge for people the world did not want and the smoke and waste the rest of London didn't want either. In modern day Newham, only 61.8 per cent of people were born in the UK (ONS 2004). It would be a cruel irony if the East End, an area historically populated by the disenfranchised would be bypassed as little more than a convenient marketing hook in the Olympic Bid.

Perception influence

In much the way that nothing that is ever *said* is not political; the same can be said for anything that is ever *seen*. Whether Britain likes it or not, to stage an event of the international magnitude of the Olympic Games, is to be perceived by the world. Britain consequently has to respond to the pragmatic need to ensure that the perception of British cultural identity received by the world is as beneficial as possible. If discovery of personal cultural identity is about the understanding of the self; influencing perceptions is concerned with helping people understand 'the other'. In this case that 'other' is other people's understanding of the East End, London, The Thames Gateway and the UK as a whole.

Tourists are often cited as one such group that can have their preferences influenced by the staging of an Olympic Games. The impact of major events on tourists, can be often overstated. Increases in inward visits to Australia in the Olympic year were by no means out of keeping with the aggregate increases during the 1990s. Since Sydney 2000, visitor numbers have actually been falling. The story for Athens however may be some what bleaker. The fact that the tickets for the Games themselves have failed to sell out suggests that securing a long term increase in tourists for Greece may be difficult to realise.

In communicating to external audiences the Olympic organisers should think less in terms of marketing the Games to international visitors, but more about winning the respect of the international community. This is more likely to achieve a longer-term sustainable legacy. Leonard and Alakeson (2000) have argued that as the flow of information and the means to communicate become increasingly democratised, it is people in other states rather than their governments, that diplomatic efforts need to be focused upon. Leonard and Alakeson (2000) argue:

We must learn to communicate with overseas publics as pro-
fessionally as with governments . . . to be successful we will
need to prove our relevance and win the trust of the people we
are communicating with . . . our broader society will often have
more capacity, expertise and credibility than the British government when it comes to successfully interacting with a key
group on a particular issue . . . Increasingly we must rely on the
power of attraction rather than coercion in our dealings with
other countries . . . with an unprecedented spread of democracy, our ability to win over governments will depend in part on
how we are perceived by the populations they serve. In this
global battle for influence the international reputation of a
country is one of its most important assets.

While simply staging the Games successfully is likely to influence the
way that Britain is perceived around the world, the cultural programme can play a pivotal role in this process.

The understanding of the self and the understanding of the other
are mutually related. If the cultural programme does not engage with
cultural activity throughout London and particularly in the East End
any attempt to bring about a perception change in the way the UK is
viewed will lack legitimacy and ultimately remain unsustainable.
This process can bridge the gap between people and a sporting festival, generating ownership of the Games throughout the nation, connecting people with what can seem like a monolithic international
circus. Closer to home it can reinforce local identity and pride in the
East End, forming the bedrock for the construction of sustainable
communities, bolstering the creative industries, engage artists and
encouraging visitors.

Cultural content

In order to fulfil the need to have meaningful cultural engagement
and alter perception in a positive light, there is a need to develop
'content' around which a cultural programme could be developed.

The ideas need to be understandable and communicable. This is different from 'dumbing down', of marketers but could give guidance to artists and creatives.

If defined too rigorously, the characteristics could alienate more people than they include, while if set very loosely as vague themes the message could simply become meaningless. I am proposing an agenda or manifesto to centralise ideas. The making then of the projects and outcomes from these ideas can be strictly left to the organisation or individual. For the cultural programme to be a success, I believe that these principles need to be applied throughout.

Projects are exploratory
The paradox outlined at the start of the piece shows that culture cannot be reduced simply to grand statements of identity. The content of the program should aim to question rather than represent a display of answers. Only in this way can culture help learning and understanding and be inclusive.

Projects are collaborative
All projects imply collaboration. This is either cross-sector, or between forms, or between industries and disciplines.

Projects are participatory
That all projects seamlessly join community, educational and creative groups.

Projects are challenging
That the content has a relevance either politically or socially.

Projects relate to different audiences
The work can be understood and read globally, and by people at different levels of society.

Our challenge will be to embed non-linear and perhaps abstract structures that will be grounded in politics, society, education and community. No one has yet achieved this, but this is the place where Britain as a nation could so imaginatively weave together the sectors of technology, heritage and art in a way that will help to decode the new millennium.

Suggestions for Cultural Programming

While not aiming to be overly proscriptive, there is a need to develop a series of ideas that provide hypothetical expressions of these ideas.

An online investigation

This could be a large, internationally accessible online resource to link all the elements of the cultural programme together and lead an investigation into its projects. Rather than functioning simply as a promotional tool for the UK it would showcase projects being conducted and provide fora to discuss the different themes being explored and questions being asked during the cultural programme. It could act as a hub for museums, television and schools to explain and discuss the work that they were doing and the meaning behind them. The website could be designed and maintained by companies from the creative industries in the Lower Lea Valley. While not having public relations as a key objective, as an international visible face of Britain at work, it could reflect positively on modern Britain and cast London as the lead global focus on new technology and its power for positive social ends.

Themes for museums

Museums would be well placed to lead an investigation of the past and contextualise it in the present. It is important for the themes used by museums to resonate at national levels but also at local levels too. It would provide an opportunity to engage with history not as objects in cases, but as the movement of energy and people, and an enriching learning experience. The themes could form the sound basis for investigatory partnership working with schools and artists drawing on practice developed by initiatives such as Creative Partnerships (an organisation that has loci in all of the Olympic boroughs).

■ *Britain joins the world*

While Britain's colonial heritage is associated with dominating the world, as the Jubilee celebrations and the Commonwealth Games showed, it has also been a place to bring it together. From Victorian railways to telephones, televisions and Tim Berners-Lee's internet, Britons have pioneered bringing different people and cultures closer together. The East End has historically been the human face of Britain's openness to the world. Since the arrival of the Huguenots at the end of the Seventeenth Century the East End has been a new home to Jews, Bangladeshis and most recently the Somali community. In London 172 languages are spoken; 125 of which are spoken in Waltham Forest and 72 in Tower Hamlets. Already developed as a key theme during the Commonwealth Games this could provide the basis for how Britain is prepared to deal with itself as a nation with a colonial past.

■ *Conflict and compassion*

Conflict takes many forms. Its resolution is a key theme in the Olympics while it has moulded the development of modern Britain and the London we know; from Cromwellian Iconoclasm, to proletarian strife and contemporary ethnic tension. The flip side of unrivalled diversity in the East End has been felt in extreme politics and racial tension. The British Union of Fascists in the 1930s, The National Front in the 1970s and the BNP in recent years have blighted the area. The East End was also heavily effected by the Blitz. While the iconic image of St. Paul's Cathedral riding over burning London is held in the popular memory it is often forgotten that it was Stepney, Poplar and Bethnal Green that bore the brunt of London's suffering.

But Britain has historically also been a place of caring. It is the home of participatory parliamentary democracy, a nationalised health service, some of the oldest schools and university's as well as being the first country to introduce compulsory education. The East End at many times has remained outside the caring of the state but has championed a self-reliance of its own. East London was home to Thomas Barnado (founder of the children's charity Barnados) and William Booth, founder of the Salvation Army. It was also home to progressive political movements. During the late Nineteenth Century Fairfield Road in Bow was home to the Suffragettes and the struggle for women's enfranchisement.

■ *Britain as a place of subculture*

During the Twentieth Century Britain granted a bigger voice to its younger generations. The collective behaviour of young people in Britain is amongst the nation's most vibrant and leaves us with new traditions in pop music, fashion and the visual arts. Yesterday's sub-culture often resembles an innovation unit for the piecemeal culture of every day life today. Without punk spiky hair wouldn't be acceptable for bank clerks; without acid house the soundtrack to the *Six O'Clock News* would not sound the same, while our usage of every day language is informed from the fringes.

ONS population projections suggest the boroughs of East London will have some of the highest concentrations of young people in the UK (www.statistics.gov.uk). At a time when the population of Britain will be collectively aging it is likely that sub-culture will thrive but is more likely to remain unseen. The image of the East End as a home to brothels, violence and gangsters popularised in Guy Richie's films belittles the contribution of London and the East End's subculture. Today it is home to new thriving scenes of its own. Dizzee Rascal winner of the Mercury Music prize in 2003 hails from Bow. While Ragga, Drum&Bass and garage all emerged from London in the 1990s. 'Grime' the supposedly 'it' sound for 2004 has also emerged from the East End.

■ *Investigating change*

The approach to the documentation and the shaping of the Olympic Bid and transformation of the Lower Lea Valley must look and feel different from a centralised Grand Aunt informing us what to look and feel. The seismic changes in the area should be documented by artists, where possible working in partnership with local schools and community groups and young people. This could form the basis for exhibitions in museums throughout the country and as a project could be incubated in the new Rich Mix centre using the formats of radio, television and cinema. It could also form the basis for the spatial and visual development in the area in the period after the Games.

■ *Exploring language*

A young people's spoken word project, using influences emergent from the East End from Shakespeare, through to hip-hop and grime we could create a global schools programme and collaborate for presentations throughout the Olympic year. The outcomes from this should link historical literature with global cultures and new cultures. The outcomes from this should support the idea that many world voices contribute via London, to the Olympics.

■ *Olympics through the margins*

The Olympics themselves could be documented on a specially designated digital TV station or radio frequency, presented and developed by local people, documenting the build up to the Games and the celebrations and events surrounding them. It could be a basis for people living in London and around the Olympic site to showcase their way of life and their own experience of the Olympics. It could have the personal feel of the BBC's *Paddington Green* or *Video Nation* but would provide a deeper snapshot of local lives.

■ *Art, science and sport*

Live artists and dance artists could work together around themes of the body, science and sport. A cross collaboration could be constructed between scientists and athletes, while schools and artists could work together to examine links between aesthetics and performance. The outcomes from this work could result in improved technological analysis of sports performance, or perhaps a basis for kit design for the British Olympic team.

Conclusion – from cultural programme to cultural project

The Olympic Games is a cultural call for answers: an unreasonable, modern demand for simplicity in a complex and fractured world. The iconography of the Games and the ceremonial help to convey this, but unless they are supported by a cultural programme that is underpinned by the principles outlined in this chapter the messages conveyed during the Games themselves will lack integrity and be prone to attack, cynicism and accusations of hypocrisy.

The cultural programme should be thought of as more of an investigation or project than a programme of the display of answers. The showmanship of answers can be left to the ceremonial of the Games themselves. If the ruling concept of all cultural programmes is to generate 'understanding' of one form or another, this will only be achievable if the programme is established with an investigatory function.

If culture is to leave a legacy of an improved understanding of both the self and the other, both the content chosen for the themes of the cultural programme and the way in which they are translated into projects is of critical importance. Only if these two issues can be addressed can the gap between people throughout the nation and a sporting festival really be made.

By the same token, these principles also relate to creating ownership between people and a transformation of their locality, regardless of whether the Games do or do not go ahead. It is consequently essential that the themes resonate with East London. The cultural programme can potentially extol the ideals and set the precedent the successful regeneration of the Lower Lea Valley.

And therein lies the importance of the Olympic Games themselves. Ultimately they should be a celebration of the bigger things going on in Britain rather than a fabricated party of distant ideals. The 'big things' by 2012 will all be there; our ages, lifestyles, technologies, our individual collective histories and futures, hopes and fears. The challenge for the cultural programme is to explore these in the years preceding the Games, rather than shoe horning them into vacuous symbolism for a seventeen-day event. If this is to be achieved it will mean that institutions will have to facilitate the experience of people. Not vicariously through Kylie, Freddy Mercury and Muhammad Ali, but in you, me, pirate radio, the artists on the fringes and the revellers of Notting Hill.

7 Conclusion: Minding the Gap

Melissa Mean,
Anthony Vigor and
Charlie Tims

7 Conclusion: Minding the Gap

Melissa Mean, Anthony Vigor and Charlie Tims

The 'greatest show on earth' requires major political, institutional, community and financial effort to pull off. Given this, it is perhaps not surprising that the prospect of hosting an Olympic Games generates such great expectations for what is a twenty nine-day event. Indeed, the chance to hold the 2012 Games in London has already generated high hopes. The claims so far include: increased sports participation and sporting success; thousands of new jobs; a boost for new business; an upturn in tourism; and ultimately, the regeneration of East London – an area suffering some of the highest levels of disadvantage in the UK.

There is nothing new about this fever of expectations surrounding an Olympic Bid. However, as the preceding chapters illustrate, past Games have not always lived up to the claims of the PR machine in terms of securing a positive long-term legacy. Past Games have tended to be used as a means of 'driving change' in the host city and its economy, with the focus and investment required to host the Games used as an opportunity to build new infrastructure and boost the local economy. There are flaws in this approach. Firstly, the top-down fast-track approach to development, encouraged by unmovable Olympic deadlines, can fail to be responsive to wider interests with a lack of ownership and connection with longer term community needs. Secondly, there is frequently a failure to embed Olympic initiatives within mainstream and ongoing local and national programmes and policies. Thirdly, the emphasis on physical infrastructure – building the necessary new sporting facilities and any transport improvements and housing required – leads to a neglect of softer social infrastructure issues. The cumulative impact of these factors is that there is frequent mismatch between the infrastructure and investment required to run a successful Games and the longer term needs of the host community, with a failure of benefits to flow to the places and people that need them most.

This kind of mismatch, and its causes, are far from unique to Olympic Games and is a phenomena that urban planners confront in every new development and regeneration programme – from the re-building of Wembley to the plan to double the size of Milton Keynes. London needs to acknowledge the potential for mismatch and address it head on. This chapter offers three guiding principles that should be at heart of any approach that seeks to close the gap, and in doing so secure both a successful Games and contribute to the long-term needs of the area. It then considers what this means for each legacy theme addressed in this report and, finally, it will offer nine policy recommendations that will help secure a sustainable legacy.

Three organising principles for a successful, sustainable Games

Running through each of these principles is the desire to bring together and secure a better interaction between physical and social infrastructure. As one expert we spoke to put it: 'Delivering the legacy will be a people issue. Do not for one minute think it will only be facilities issue.'

Embedding the Olympics in mainstream programmes

One of the strongest themes to emerge from our research and the authors of the preceding chapters, is that on its own an Olympics will not deliver a beneficial, sustainable legacy. If a London 2012 Olympics is to deliver a sustainable legacy, it will be vital to embed the Olympics within broader programmes and policy agendas that start well before 2012 and continue well afterwards.

This does not hold for just national and regional policy. It will also be vital to embed Olympic initiatives with the significant number of locally-delivered programmes. The table in Appendix 1 identifies a number of initiatives that are already up-and-running within the Olympic boroughs. If handled appropriately the Olympics could help these initiatives to deliver on their own objectives. In this way concern that a 2012 London Olympics might capture or divert some funding from established programmes could be assuaged. Equally, by using a London 2012 Olympics to contribute towards core local agendas of employment, active communities, liveability and improved local services would strengthen the Bid by encouraging community buy-in through making clearer links with people's everyday lives.

Strategic use of the Olympics Effect

The Olympics has leverage. Repeatedly in interviews with individuals involved with previous bids – both failed and successful – we were told that an Olympics like nothing else mobilises interest, people and resources. The most visible evidence of this is the billions of television viewers and the most expensive broadcast deal in the world. It is also in evidence in the blue-chip firms queuing up to get their brand alongside the Five Rings. Less visibly, the Olympics Effect is also felt in the people signing up to volunteer and the new working relationships between a wide variety of public, private and civic sector organisations in the host cities and more widely. For example, people in Manchester frequently cite the most important legacy from the two failed Olympic bids and the 2002 Commonwealth Games is the way it has fostered a collaborative relationship between the public and private sectors.

London needs to be smart about how it strategically deploys the Olympics Effect to help secure a sustainable legacy. According to IOC insiders, since London's lacklustre third place behind Paris and Madrid following the initial shortlist of bidding cities in March, London has made impressive progress and now its bid is regarded as the best technically. But, as a number of the chapters point out the barriers to really good performance are not just technical, but also institutional, behavioural and financial. The one-off nature of the Olympics combined with its 'mobiliser effect' creates an opportunity to suspend some elements of 'business as usual' which hinder, for example, the achievement of higher environmental quality and higher rates of sports participation. In the process, the Olympics can demonstrate that a different way is possible and build up the necessary skills, experience and capacity to change assumptions and patterns of behaviour for the long term. There is no reason why this effect has to be restricted to the host community, and could be felt both nationally and internationally in certain areas.

However, it is unrealistic to expect an Olympics to make the whole world anew; it will not be a cure-all. It will therefore be important to use the Olympics Effect in a targeted and strategic way and not let it leak away. For example, the new infrastructure developments should set new environmental standards that would not only deliver environmental benefits, but also serve as a demonstration to other areas of the UK and the world of what is possible and do it in a way that helps build UK green industry capacity.

Importantly, the process can and must start now – there is a potential dividend to be won from the bidding process itself. As in Manchester there is a sense that the bidding process brought together different groups to think about the future of the area in a way that is probably unprecedented. A number of people we spoke to claimed that five London Olympic boroughs are working together in a collaborative way that has not been witnessed before. This is welcome and necessary. The cost of the bidding process itself – £30 million – demands that it delivers some lasting benefits itself.

Investing in community capacity and ownership
A vital part of securing greater public value from the Olympics means getting closer to what the public actually values by creating opportunities for community involvement, ownership and leadership. As many of the chapters argued, for the Games to deliver a lasting positive legacy, people must feel part of the process. Not only will local residents want demonstrable employment and housing benefits and access to any new sports facilities as soon as possible, they will also need to be able to actively shape and contribute to their on-going planning and design. Without this level of engagement there is a danger that the new developments will not be relevant to their needs or

sustainable once the Olympics circus has left town. As one community organiser put it: 'We don't want the Olympics done to us, we want to be involved.'

Participation rarely works if it is top down and last minute. Nor does it work if people are merely consulted on what has already been decided upon elsewhere. The pace of the Olympic Master Planning Process and Bid campaign can seem breathless. Deadlines for planning applications, environmental assessments, submitting the Bid Book, building the stadiums and so on can become excuses for not including people, or a perennial reason to defer greater participation until some later date.

London 2012 has shown that it is sensitive to these issues. They have run an initial community consultation programme, established a London 2012 Forum, a London 2012 Environmental Advisory Group and established a Legacy Board. Despite this, however, it is still unclear exactly how local people will participate in a deeper way than consultation and representative forums can provide. The failures of the New Deal for Communities and Neighbourhood Renewal Fund, as highlighted by Mike Raco, must not be repeated by a London Olympics. One way to approach the Olympics is to see it as part of a longer term community capacity building process. A critical issue that this process needs to address is ensuring that some of the value from rising land prices and development in the area is captured for community benefit. Equally, development will need to guard against regeneration resulting in the replacement of one population with another as existing residents are forced to move out by rising housing and living costs.

What does this mean for each legacy theme?

Social legacy

There are three main social policy areas where the Olympics needs to be embedded: affordable housing, transport and strengthening the public realm.

Housing policy at both the national and regional scale is important. The London Plan (Mayor of London 2004) stipulated that all new housing developments must contain fifty per cent affordable housing, of which seventy per cent should be social housing (landlord-provided rental, where rents are at or below government target levels) and thirty per cent intermediate (sub-market, affordable to households on incomes less than £40,000). In the 2004 Spending Review, the chancellor also announced an extra 10,000 social rented homes by 2008. The provision of affordable housing – arguably, especially social rented – will be very important in helping to ensure that existing residents are not forced to leave the area because of rising house prices.

In transport, community benefit should be the key determinant. Despite media and IOC reservations, it seems as though the Bid Team have developed a robust transport plan to meet a Games' requirements. Whether Crossrail is built in time or not, is a diversion. It is neither necessary for the Olympics, nor will it leave a significant local community legacy in the Lower Lea Valley. Rather, the welcome East London Line extension, other light rail improvements and even more importantly, buses, are the ways in which local residents – especially those on lower incomes – are likely to access employment and travel around London (Grayling 2001). Within the Lower Lea Valley area comprehensive and accessible walking and cycling networks will be the key to securing community benefit, particularly given the lower than average car ownership levels in the area.

Strengthening the public realm relates to two connected policy areas: civic participation and active communities. The Government has set a target to increase 'voluntary and community engagement, especially amongst those at risk of social exclusion' (HMT 2004a) and has also established the Russell Commission to investigate opportunity of establishing a National Youth Volunteering Strategy (HMT 2004b). It is generally assumed to be a 'good thing' if people are active as volunteers, participate in democratic life or are involved in shaping the future of their local communities. But as Stanley (2004) argues: 'there are very few public policy levers available [to increase levels of civic engagement] so we have to maximise the use of those that do appear to be promising.'

In terms of the public realm, the Olympics offers a potentially significant extra policy lever and should be embraced as such. Two areas stand out in particular.

First, the Olympics relies upon the work of an army of volunteers, and, so large is the pool required, this could include volunteers from across the UK. However, as Fred Coalter's chapter identifies, past major sporting events have not been effective at engaging people other than those who tend to be active anyway. Engaging people beyond the usual suspects and in particular 'hard to reach' groups will be a key priority for the London Olympics. As in Manchester through its Pre-Volunteer Programme, volunteers should receive training and support that enhances their skills. However, past volunteer programmes have focused too much on trying to enhance individuals' employment prospects. While this may be an outcome of an individuals' involvement, it should not be the prime objective. Rather, the Olympics should focus on contributing towards a sustainable volunteering and civic engagement agenda more usefully. Reducing the emphasis on getting skills for jobs, may open up more diverse and creative ways to engage a broader range of people.

Second, as Mike Raco's chapter argued, the neighbourhood renewal agenda's civic participation has been criticised for simultaneously over consulting residents and leaving them with a sense that they have little real control over any development. Given the amount of development planned in the Lower Lea Valley – whether the Games are held or not – there is likely to be significant local community interest, the challenge is to ensure participation does not suffer this same fate. This will require a number of issues to be addressed:

■ A long-term perspective is essential if integrated approaches to civic participation and inclusion are to be sustainable. 2012 seems like a long way off, but rather than treating this date as a one-off deadline by which time all communities should somehow be uniformly engaged and active, 2012 should be treated as one milestone on a longer term programme of community capacity building, both before and after the Games themselves.

- 2012 and the Olympic stakeholder organisations need to recognise that there will be no sustainable change in the area unless communities themselves are given the power and responsibility to take action. An important part of achieving this will be securing some of the land and facilities in the Lower Lea Valley for community benefit and ownership. The considerable land bank that the London Development Agency has built up over the past eighteen months in the Lower Lea Valley offers an opportunity to put at least some of the land and facilities required for the Games aside for community enterprise. A diversity of development paths should be supported over an extended period of time, including development trusts, social enterprises and neighbourhood management trusts.

- Participation requires resources. Different communities will have different needs, different aspirations and be at different stages of organisation. The physical infrastructure investment going into the area needs to be complemented with funds for community capacity building, including training and grants for feasibility studies and business plans.

Employment legacy

The Government has identified full employment in every region as one of its major priorities. While it does not provide a quantifiable definition of full employment,[1] it does identify that increasing the employment rate amongst 'disadvantaged groups' as a specific target. These are defined as lone parents, ethnic minorities, people aged fifty or over, those with the lowest qualifications and those living in the local authority wards with the poorest initial labour market position (HMT 2004a). A significant number of residents in the Olympic boroughs, and the Olympic boroughs themselves, fall into this category. If a London 2012 Games were to contribute towards regeneration in the Lower Lea Valley, then new employment opportunities created in the pre- and post-Games periods must be open residents who are economically inactive (and not simply those who are already in employment).

To achieve an increase in the employment rate amongst these disadvantaged groups may well require the prevailing 'job first' active labour market policies to be balanced by a more 'human capital' approach that provides significant training programmes specifically aimed at disadvantaged jobseekers (Robinson, forthcoming). Given the skill levels and high proportion of those who have never worked within the Olympic boroughs, it is clear that if these residents are to secure employment opportunities, they are likely to need sufficient training before the job openings appear. The Government are conducting two reforms that are important here. First, New Deal policies are being reformed towards 'local solutions meeting individual needs', where greater emphasis and effort is placed upon understanding and meeting the needs of both benefit claimants and employers (DWP 2004). Second, and relatedly, the benefits and employment services are being merged into the new Jobcentre Plus network, which will also work in more detail with individual clients to help them into and retain work (Jobcentre Plus 2003).

As Martin Crookston argued in his chapter, if the economically inactive in the Olympic boroughs (and in other London boroughs) are to benefit from any new employment opportunities, then a lot of detailed work will be required to match both demand (employers' needs) and supply-side (individuals') needs. Otherwise, employers' perceptions of unemployed individuals in East London may mean they look to hire elsewhere. Also, disadvantaged individuals may well be 'out competed' for new employment opportunities by those with better skills travelling from further afield. This is a key challenge because securing employment benefits for local residents is a central aspect of the broader regeneration objective.

There are two other issues that must be addressed here. First, a policy tool sometimes used to deliver local employment benefit is a 'local labour agreement', where employers on big development projects have to ensure specific levels of employment and apprenticeship programmes go to local residents. These may well be useful schemes in delivering local employment benefits, but will not be enough on their own. There need to be other proactive measures to ensure that the new employment opportunities provided in the area do not simply go to those already in employment. More detailed training work will need to be conducted before the employment opportunities are available to ensure previously unemployed individuals can access them.

Second, what do we mean by 'local'? This is an important issue as London as a whole functions as one labour market and all residents will pay a Council Tax precept if London hosts the 2012 Games. Certainly, all Londoners (and under EU regulations, any EU resident) should be able to access the employment opportunities. However, as new employment is central to regeneration this must be balanced with the need to provide opportunities to the residents of the Olympic boroughs. The precise level of any 'local labour agreement' is a decision that must be made in consultation with the range of stakeholders. But there are recent examples of good practice in Greenwich that could be drawn on (both in hiring and new apprenticeship schemes). Moreover, it should be recognised that companies are keen to be associated with the Olympics and may be more inclined to agree to higher levels than has been the case in the past.

Environmental legacy

The Government is currently reviewing both its sustainable development strategy and climate change programme and due to publish new ones next year. However, the big target to meet will still stand: cutting carbon dioxide emissions amongst developed nations by sixty per cent. Climate change is increasingly being recognised as the most serious long-term threat facing the future of the planet and to respond effectively involves a whole suite of policy areas from flood risk and transport, to renewable energy and construction. A sustainable environmental legacy for London's Games should consist of going beyond the minimum of a one-off greening of the Olympic site and facilities. Instead, the Games should be used to boost the UK's capacity to close the gap between the well-known targets and a UK-wide ability to actually deliver on them on the ground. As Roger Levett highlights in his chapter, this challenge is less a technical one and more a matter of breaking through cultural and institutional inertia.

The difficulty of ensuring that efforts to stage a green Olympics are felt longer and more widely than during the Games themselves are highlighted by Sydney's experience and it provides clear lessons to London about the importance of embedding any green innovations in wider processes and programmes. Sydney's greatest success was probably the piloting and use of a fleet of gas powered buses to transport participants and spectators around Homebush Bay. Gas powered buses are now the standard bus servicing the whole of the Sydney area. Less successful in spreading beyond the Olympic zone were the (at the time) high environmental standards for reducing energy and water use in the Olympic Village and other facilities. Four years on and a quite a battle later, the state legislature has finally mandated that all new developments in the state will now have to conform to the same Olympic standards. Part of the lag, and cause for continued doubts over whether the state will be able to deliver on its new legislation, is the lack of skilled architects, designers and construction workers; the failure to mainstream these skills and development standards after the Games were over meant that the necessary expertise leaked away.

A key part of the Olympics Effect is the sheer size of the event and as such it has the ability to 'make' new products or those that so far have so far faltered at near market readiness. A scan of the near horizon reveals a host of eager candidates to help substantiate an image of Britain that is bright and green. Roger Levett's chapter provides many good ideas, and others to add to the list include: green and brown roofs, micro renewable power generators, permeable paving, hydrogen power, and natural air-conditioning building methods. Beyond individual products, the Olympics should be used to trial wider environmental processes – delivering at the scale of an Olympics the processes could then be rolled out to the wider London and Thames Gateway area, and other areas in the UK. Closed loop waste systems (as being developed by London Remade) and restoring the waterways for transport (starting with construction material and waste for the Games) would both have long lasting legacies.

The other important legacy to come from an Olympics comes from the IOC's own stated ambition – that hosting a Games should have 'no net negative impact on the environment'. Avoiding and minimising negative environmental impacts of the development and running of the Games should of course be the first priority, however, substitution offers a way to not only compensate for unavoidable impacts, but also to distribute, where appropriate, the environmental substitutions (or benefits) at a national or even international level. As a global event, there is both logic and duty that the legacy from an Olympics Games should have some global reach. A systematic and innovative programme for assessing impacts (for example, greenhouse gas emissions generated by those flying to the Games) and a way of substituting them would be a worthwhile legacy not only for a London 2012 Games, but future Games to come.

Sport

For a sustainable sporting legacy, the focus of effort must be on using a London Olympic Games to promote increased participation across the UK. This must be across a range of sports, not just official Olympics sports. Participation rates have been falling in recent years, with the decline in participation most pronounced amongst the younger age groups (also see Rowe and Moore, 2004). These trends are well recognised within government and the national sporting bodies (for example, see Sport England, 2004a). *Game Plan* (DCMS/Cabinet Office, 2002) set an aspirational target of '70% (currently ~30%) of the population to be reasonably active (for example 30 minutes of moderate exercise five times a week) by 2020.' To achieve this will require a significant amount of effort and resources dedicated towards grassroots sports. All the national sports councils have recently adopted strategies towards achieving this (Sports Council for Wales, 2004; Sport England, 2004b; **sport**scotland, 2003; NIGD 2002).

As Fred Coalter argues, it is very difficult to isolate an 'Olympic effect' in sports participation levels. Specific 'Olympic targets' for sports would therefore be misplaced. However, the prospect of a London Olympics does highlight the need for those involved in sports policy to reach out to new communities and participants, understanding and providing for their needs. As Fred argues, this should start now.

Schools and local authorities will be important in delivering a sustainable legacy. Early schemes such as free swimming for children in the Olympic boroughs are encouraging but must be part of a broader, sustained agenda. There is no need to wait until the 2005 hosting decision; the hope of hosting the Games should be used to generate increased interest for sports participation. Further, as soon as any of the Olympic facilities are completed, they should be available for community use, not closed until after the Games. The local community must feel part of the Games before, during and after the event.

Sports' national governing bodies must also play a key role. The Rugby Football Union's (RFU) IMPACT[2] strategy is an interesting approach to converting the increased interest a major event can provide into sustained increases in participation and retention in playing, coaching, officiating and administration (RFU 2003). Because the strategy was publicly launched in September 2003, there is no data yet on the success of the programme. The approach, however, seems sound. IMPACT recognises the need for different strategies before, during and after an event and that a significant amount of the work required to secure sustainable legacies occurs before the major event itself. This goes beyond the provision of new facilities. For example, as part of a broader programme, the RFU helped 2,000 people qualify as coach-referees in junior aspects of the game, accredited 4,000 new referees, established 2,600 club/school links and provided resources and advice on increasing the number of schools playing rugby.

The London Olympics also has the opportunity to take innovative approaches to sports participation one step further and integrate it with health, environmental and social agendas. There is a growing body of evidence that shows that sustained participation in sport and exercise is greatest when the activity also has a perceived social or environmental value for the individual taking part (RSPB forthcoming). The enthusiasm of the lone individual driving to the gym generally fades much quicker than those involved in green gyms (conservation and gardening clubs), walking groups or running clubs using accessible, high quality green space. The design brief for the Olympic site and subsequent development should have at its core imaginative principles to design in the ease and desirability of more active lifestyles for people living and working in the area.

Cultural legacy

As outlined in Keith Khan's chapter, the purpose of culture is to increase better understanding of ourselves and of one another. If the cultural dimension of the Olympics is to be sustainable it must leave a lasting legacy that increases our capacity to do this.

From a user's perspective the cultural sector is characteristically fractured in the UK with a lack of connections between libraries, museums, galleries, the media environment, science centers, theatres, archives and creative spaces. The Cultural Programme provides an opportunity to conduct a series of projects that build lasting links between these organisations, and generates new relationships with individuals, families, schools and community groups.

If the cultural sector is to further dissolve the divide between institutions and audiences it will be important for the programme to draw on the practice of organisations and bodies that have already built relationships between the cultural sector and elsewhere. The work of Creative Partnerships for example, which has a strong presence in the capital, provides good examples of building innovative relationships between the cultural sector and schools.

In continuation of the themes of widening participation and access as outlined in the DCMS's *Culture and Creativity: the next ten years* (2001) a cultural programme that emphasises participation increases the opportunities for cultural organisations to cement their position in their localities. The new Rich Mix centre in Bethnal Green would potentially be well positioned to utilise a cultural programme to embed itself in this way.

In an international context the Olympics presents opportunities for towns, local authorities and villages throughout the UK to bolster and construct new relationships that they already have with places overseas, through twinning programmes. Such relationships could be developed by the cultural programme during the games, while forming the basis for school and professional exchanges after it.

Ultimately, as suggested in Keith's chapter, if the games are to leave a sustainable legacy for the cultural sector and those affected by it, the games will need to set a benchmark for taking as wide a definition of culture as possible seeing beyond, racial and class divides.

Nine ideas for a sustainable London 2012 Olympics

Is the race to win the right to host an Olympic Games worth winning? The premise of this report is that it is only worth winning if the Games secure a sustainable legacy and the benefits flow to the people and places most in need. The evidence shows that there is no automatic Olympic dividend for host cities and countries. Instead, a sustainable legacy depends upon Olympic related infrastructure, investment and initiatives being embedded with wider policy objectives and programmes – both before the seventeen-day event and afterwards. What might this mean in practice? The preceding chapters offer a wide range of concrete suggestions. Complementing and building on these, the rest of this conclusion offers nine practical recommendations for London to help secure a sustainable legacy. They are designed to benefit a range of different constituencies – including local people in the immediate vicinity of the main Olympic site and communities across the UK. They look to extending the legacy benefits outside the UK; as argued above, the Olympics is a global event and there is a logic and duty for the legacy of a London Games to have a global reach. The recommendations also extend over a range of timescales – some could and should begin now, and all have a life long after 2012.

Community Enterprise Endowment Fund

A fund should be established that complements the physical infrastructure investment in the Lower Lea Valley with social infrastructure development. This could be funded through hypothecating a proportion of the sponsorship deals a London Games would strike and seeking additional sponsorship from the family of existing Olympic sponsors. The fund should be focused on developing capacity in community-based organisations and entrepreneurs to develop at least a proportion of the land assembled and facilities built for the Olympics. The fund should be made available for business plans, feasibility studies and training. This should be an incremental process beginning before the Games and continuing afterwards. The overall aim should be develop the Lower Lea Valley as a hub for social enterprise and alternative development models – and it already has a strong base of these from which to grow.

Off-Setting Programme

To ensure a positive environmental legacy and meet the IOC's challenge of no negative net impact on the environment, London should develop an off-setting programme for the environmental impacts that cannot be avoided. This will require identifying and recording different impacts (everything from increased water consumption to greenhouse gas emissions from people flying to the Games), devising suitable substitutions and monitoring their implementation. Some of these impacts will be local and should be substituted locally, others have a global scale impact and could be substituted at an international level. This could provide a non-tokenistic way to spread the legacy outside London and in particular to developing countries. Such a programme and the system to run also serve future Olympic Games.

Substitutions could include:

- Funding renewable energy development programmes in developing countries. This should add to efforts to speed up dissemination of renewable technologies – a key challenge identified at the 2004 Bonn International Conference for Renewable Energies.

- As a contribution towards the Government's commitment that by 2016–2018 nobody in Britain should be living in fuel poverty, there could be investment in 'warm zones' in the five Olympic boroughs. Increased energy use constructing and hosting the

Games could be off-set by a programme to insulate existing housing stock in the surrounding areas. Alongside the environmental legacy, this would also have a significant social legacy by targeting those households suffering from fuel poverty and provide a very tangible way for people living in the area to feel that the Olympics was benefiting local residents. This initiative would augment the existing Warm Zone programme in Newham and shortly to be expanded to other areas.

The off-setting programme should be funded by a levy on all flights coming into London airports for the duration of the Games and one week either side. Such a levy set at £20 per passenger would raise nearly £120 million.[3]

Employment Taskforce

An Olympic Employment Taskforce should be established. It would draw on the model already developed for the Jobcentre Plus Rapid Response Service – where a range of relevant stakeholders work in partnership to help redeploy those facing job losses in major redundancies. However, instead of reacting to major job loss and trying to place redundant workers in new employment, the taskforce would work with employers to proactively identify new employment opportunities and the needs of unemployed individuals in accessing them. It should also be led by the London Development Agency. As the Mayor's job agency it has the ability to identify London-wide employment opportunities and work with relevant stakeholders.

Representatives of the Job Centre Plus districts and the Learning and Skills Councils that cover the Olympic boroughs should be on the taskforce. Through this more planned and co-ordinated approach, job seekers could receive training for up-coming employment opportunities that have been identified through close collaboration with employers. This would help ensure that when new employment opportunities appeared the economically inactive of the Olympic boroughs were not routinely 'out-competed' by better skilled workers travelling from across the South East.

The Street Olympics

The Street Olympics would be an opportunity for people across the UK to design and compete in their own neighbourhood-based Games; thus the UK would not have just one Olympics Games, but hundreds up and down the country. These festival events could be organised by pubs, community centres, local charities, faith organisations, resident groups and neighbours in streets, schools, youth clubs, sports clubs. The events would include sporting and non-sporting events – everything from the long jump and the 400 metres to sack-races and frisbee-throwing contests. This will provide a chance for people who are good at traditional sports and those that are not to participate equally. Street Olympics should be supported with an information pack and website (organisations like Bristol's *Streets Alive!* already run a successful scheme for street festivals with advice on everything from getting insurance to getting streets closed, and the ODPM and Sport England (2004) *Street Games* initiative also provides a similarly useful example). Street Olympics could be as small as neighbours competing in their back gardens, to a full-blown festival with stalls and sponsorship. The legacy of the Street Olympics would lie in people getting to know their neighbours, organisations working together who had not before, and in helping create lively neighbourhoods and a positive community memory.

The Street Olympics could take place before the main Games in August 2012, or during it. One option might be to tie them in with an event like Comic Relief or Sport Relief. Alternatively, the Street Olympics could be linked with a suitable TV show – for example, they could become the next generation version of *Blue Peter*'s famously successful 'bring and buy' sales.

Codifying a healthy city

London 2012 and others have already spoken about creating a 'Sport City' in the Lower Lea Valley. Facilities alone are not enough. Nor should sport be treated in isolation from other forms of exercise and everyday activity. The design brief for the Olympic site and subsequent development should set bold and imaginative standards for encouraging the ease and desirability of more active lifestyles for people living and working in the area. Enhancing green space in the area is already a high priority in the master plan; this should be underpinned by prioritising walking, cycling and river networks as the next essential infrastructure. Prioritising walking, cycling, river transport and active life-styles should also be used to connect the Olympic site with the surrounding areas, and something that the five Olympic boroughs could begin to prioritise now, for example through investing in cycle routes, home zones, and prioritising pedestrians. Thirty years ago Copenhagen began its gradual transformation into one of the most cycling and walking friendly cities in the world through a deliberate programme led by the city council. Through a coordinated effort, using the Olympics as a pump-primer, the five Olympic boroughs could in a similar timeframe (or even less) be the best place to walk, cycle and play sport in the UK.

International Olympic Corps

A long-term volunteer programme for people wanting to take a year out from work, higher education or between career moves. This would represent a practical application of the Olympic values focused on the harmonious development of humankind and internationalism. Volunteers would sign up to one or more years to work on an Olympic themed project in another country, ideally the exchange would be between developed and less developed countries (in either direction). Reflecting the three Olympic pillars, volunteers could work on cultural, sport or environmental programmes. The programme could be delivered in partnership with an established programme such as GAP or VSO.

Volunteer Programme Plus

The Olympics relies upon an army of volunteers to ensure that the Games function. Evidence from past Games shows that significant numbers of people want to contribute to hosting the 'greatest show on earth'. This enthusiasm should be tapped through a Pre-Games Volunteer Programme that contributes towards the broader active communities agenda. Volunteers should serve 'Olympic apprenticeships' at local clubs, groups and societies in the run-up to the Games. This would give volunteers valuable practical experience as well as help meet volunteering shortfalls. Volunteers could come from across the UK – so similar programmes should be run across the UK's nations and regions as appropriate.

After the Games are held, a database of those volunteers who would like to continue their volunteering activity should be kept by an appropriate body in the relevant UK nation or region. Clubs, groups and societies could identify any volunteering shortfalls and these could be matched to volunteers' interests to help contribute towards a legacy of increased voluntary activity.

An annual National School Olympics

Building upon existing school sports competitions and 'youth Olympics', a national 'School Olympics' could be held every year in the run up to and beyond the 2012 Olympic Games. Schools would compete in individual sports (not only Olympic) initially on a regional basis. Regional finalists should then play in a national competition held over one weekend. To encourage a sense of national ownership of the new facilities, once they are built they should be used as the national finals venues where appropriate. In the year of the Games, the finals could be used as the test events for the facilities (with free ticketing).

A cultural resource for open learning

The entire Cultural Programme should be conducted through an electronic hub that offers a place to discuss, interrogate and affect the shape of the projects and themes that it contains. When the cultural programme is completed, the website should sow the seeds of what will become a national gateway to the UK's cultural resources. Building on the networks and knowledge developed during the cultural programme, the electronic resource would provide access to information held throughout organisations in the cultural sector. For starters, this resource could provide a hub for the following:

- Nationally index all exhibitions, theatrical productions, screenings, club listings, festivals, concerts and carnivals being held throughout the UK.

- Register learning courses, workshops and opportunities run by the cultural institutions and organisations throughout the UK.

- Provide pathways to library databases and archive resources.

- Provide a clearing-house for opportunities for individuals, schools and community organisations to collaborate with artists and cultural institutions.

- Provide support, opportunities and information for people of all ages wanting to develop careers in the cultural sector and develop a directory for different professional development opportunities.

- Provide spaces for artists and creative professionals of all backgrounds to use the resource as a means to generate and showcase their work; providing music downloads, virtual exhibitions and conduct open source projects.

The site could provide a passport to every Briton, for their own personal cultural empowerment, experience and learning while at the same time building networks and links between a disparate cultural and creative sector. The resource could build not only on the work conducted during the Cultural Programme but also on a spectrum of current initiatives such as Culture Online, BBC Blast, Creative Partnerships and Regional Cultural Consortiums. The hub could be prototyped in the East End, possibly centered in the Rich Mix centre before being expanded as a national initiative throughout the UK.

Endnotes

Chapter 1

1   It is recognised that the correct name is the Olympic Games and Paralympic Games. However, to avoid repetition of this wordy title, 'Olympics' or 'Olympic Games' will be used throughout this report.

2   A detailed breakdown for how this figure has been arrived at is unavailable. This has been criticised by the House of Commons' Select Committee on Culture, Media and Sport (HofC 2003).

3   It should also be noted that the UK has a similar example. Sheffield is still servicing a debt incurred in hosting the 1991 World Student Games. Some have suggested this is costing city council tax payers £25 million a year (LibDems 2004).

4   The sports legacy was not included as an aim; this was left to Sport England to deliver.

Chapter 2

1   An audit of the Sydney Games estimated that the event had generated AUS$3 billion worth of business outcomes, an injection of AUS$6 billion worth of infrastructure spending, and a further AUS$6 billion in inbound tourism spending (PricewaterhouseCoopers 2001).

2   As Dorling and Thomas' (2004) study shows Hackney and Tower Hamlets are at the bottom of league tables for social deprivation. Poverty in Newham, for example, has risen by 13 per cent between 1991–2001 – the fastest rate of increase anywhere in the UK.

3   It is worth noting that since 1995 most community-based projects require a percentage of their expenditure to be given over to 'community capacity-building measures', as yet with indifferent success (see Raco 2003).

4   For example, in Shoreditch, Hackney, a ten-year £180 million NDC programme was launched in February 2000. The projects have been dogged by controversy over the extent to which social housing should be promoted over and above new, commercially-oriented developments. Local community groups rejected a proposal to change their tenure from council-run to a housing association and in response the Government withheld £20 million on the grounds of the local community coming up with a policy proposal that was counter to government policy (see Weaver 2001).

5   It should be noted that there will also be significant post-Games development.

6   For example, an official opinion poll shows that eighty two per cent of Londoners support the bid.

7   These will include national government, the London Development Agency (and the Mayor), the new Thames Gateway Urban Development Corporation, local authorities, and existing development partnerships. To deliver the Olympics a raft of new agencies will be also created including an Olympic Development Agency, an Olympic Transport Agency and an Operational Command Unit (Arup 2002).

8   Some have expressed concern that the expected income from Lottery Games is over optimistic. In addition, voluntary organisations, such as the NCVO (2004) are concerned that existing Lottery money for good causes may be diverted to an Olympic Games, thereby reducing the amount available for other causes.

9   Overall ticket sales are expected to raise US$415 million

10   The Northern Way, and muted Midlands Way, are interesting developments in this regard. It is notable, however, that the Northern Way has not received any extra funding as yet.

Chapter 3

1   Although all three of these venues would be used in a 2012 Games, for football, tennis and archery, respectively.

2   Earlier research published by the Department of Social Security (1997) suggests this is true across the whole of the UK as well.

3   The London-Stansted-Cambridge growth corridor was announced as part of the Government's Sustainable Communities Plan (ODPM 2003).

Chapter 7

1   Burkitt and Robinson (2001) offer a useful working definition based upon historical analysis of an ILO unemployment rate of four per cent and over eighty per cent of the working age population in employment.

2   IMPACT stands for: Inclusion, Modernisation, Participation, Appropriate facilities, Club/school links and Training and coaching.

3   This calculation is based on the passengers arriving at all London airports in August 2003 – 5,573,211 passengers (Civil Aviation Authority 2004).

References

Chapter 1

Andranovitch G, Burbank MJ and Heying CH (2001) 'Olympic Cities: lessons learned from mega-event politics' *Journal of Urban Affairs* 23.2, 113-131

Arthur Andersen (2000) *The Sydney Olympic Performance Survey: the Sydney Olympic Games on the Australian Hotel Industry* Accessed online: www.hotelbenchmark.com/OlympicSurvey.pdf

Briggs R, McCarthy H and Zorbas A (2004) *16 Days* Demos

Brunet F (1995) 'An economic analysis of the Barcelona '92 Olympic Games: resources, financing and impact' in de Moragas Spa M and Botella M (eds) *The Keys of Success: The social, sporting, economic and communications impact of Barcelona '92* Bellaterra: Servei de Publicacions de la Universitat Autònoma de Barcelona

Buck N, Gordon I, Hull P, Marloe M and Kleinman M (2002) *Working Capital: Life and labour in contemporary London* Routledge

Chalkley B and Essex S (1999a) 'The Green Games?' *Geography* 84.4, 299-307

Chalkley B and Essex S (1999b) 'Urban Development Through Hosting International events: A history of the Olympic Games' *Planning Perspectives* 14, 369-394

Cochrane A, Peck J and Tickell A (2002) 'Olympic dreams: visions of partnership' in Peck J and Ward K (eds) *City of Revolution: restructuring Manchester* Manchester University Press, 95-115

Colville R (2004) The Business of the Olympics: From 'big owe' to pure profit *The Observer* 15.8.04

Cushman, Wakefield Healey and Baker (2003) *European Cities Monitor 2003*

Daly E and Fickling D (2002) Barcelona and Sydney: The hosts who got the most *The Observer* 8.12.02

Department for Culture, Media and Sport/Cabinet Office (DCMS/Cabinet Office) (2002) *Game Plan: A strategy for delivering Government's sport and physical activity objectives* Strategy Unit.

Department for Education and Skills (DfES) (2003a) *Primary School (Key Stage 2) Performance Tables 2003* Accessed online: www.dfes.gov.uk/performance tables/

Department for Education and Skills (DfES) (2003a) *Secondary School (Key Stage 3) Performance Tables 2003* Accessed online: www.dfes.gov.uk/performancetables/

Fauber Maunsell with Vision Consulting and Roger Tyms and Partners (2004) *Commonwealth Games Benefits Study: final report to the North West Development Agency* Accessed online: www.nwda-cms.net/DocumentUploads/CGamesReport.pdf

French SP and Disher ME (1997) Atlanta and the Olympics: A one year retrospective *Journal of the American Planning Association* 63.3, 379-392

Gratton C, Dobson N and Shibli S (2000) The Economic Importance of Major Sports Events: A case-study of six events *Managing Leisure* 5, 17-28

Greater London Authority and London Health Commission (GLA and LHC) (2003) *Health in London: Review of the London Healthy Strategy high level indicators (2003 update)* Accessed online: www.londonshealth.gov.uk/hinl2003.htm

Harvey D (1989) From Managerialism to Entrepreneurialism: The transformation in urban governance in late capitalism *Geografiska Annaler B* 71.1, 3-17

House of Commons Select Committee on Culture, Media and Sport (HofC) (2003) *A London Olympic Bid for 2012. Third Report, 2002-03 Session* Accessed online: www.publications.parliament.uk/pa/cm200203/cmselect/cmcumeds/268/26803.htm

International Olympic Committee (IOC) (2003) *Olympic Charter* Accessed online: www.multimedia.olympic.org/pdf/en_report_122.pdf

Keith M (2003) *London's Olympic Bid – Good news for the Thames Gateway* Accessed online: www.thames-gateway.org.uk/news/newsrels/2003/2003-05-16.shtml

Lesse R (2003) *Regeneration Story: The Commonwealth Games and lessons learned* Social Market Foundation.

Liberal Democrats (2004) *Sheffield on the Road to Ruin* Accessed online: www.libdems.force9.co.uk/press/2004/jun/21.htm

Livingstone K (2003) *London's Olympic Bid – Good news for the Thames Gateway* Accessed online: www.thames-gateway.org.uk/news/newsrels/2003/2003-05-16.shtml

Loftman P and Spirou CS (1996) Sports, Stadiums and Urban Regeneration: The British and United States experience *Paper presented at the Tourism and Culture: towards the 21st century conference* Longhirst Hall, Northumberland, UK 14-19 September 1996

London 2012 (2004a) *New Businesses and Jobs, Homes and Facilities* Accessed online: www.london2012.org/en/bid/regeneration

London 2012 (2004b) *Why London?* Accessed online: www.london2012.org/en/bid/WhyLondon.htm

MacKay M and Plumb C (2001) *Reaching Beyond Gold: The impact of the Olympic Games on real estate markets* Accessed online: www.joneslanglasalle.com

Mayor of London (2004) *The London Plan: Spatial development strategy for Greater London* GLA

Mahne C (2004) Did the Sydney Olympics pay off? *BBC News* Accessed online: www.news.bbc.co.uk/2/hi/business/3549580

McNulty T (2003) *London's Olympic Bid – Good news for the Thames Gateway* Accessed online: www.thames-gateway.org.uk/news/newsrels/2003/2003-05-16.shtml

MORI (2004) *The Sports Development Impact of the Commonwealth Games 2002: Final report* MORI

National Statistics (ONS) (2004a) *Regional Trends 38* Accessed online: www.statistics.gov.uk/downloads/theme_compendia/Regional_Trends_38/rt38.pdf

National Statistics (ONS) (2004b) *Census 2001: Key statistics for urban areas in the South East* TSO

National Statistics (ONS) (2004c) First Release: Qualifications and participation in learning at a local level England 2002/03 *National Statistics Release* 11.5.04 Accessed online: www.dfes.gov.uk

National Statistics (ONS) (2004d) Client Group Analysis: Quarterly bulletin – the population of working age on key benefits, November 2003 *National Statistics Release* 17.3.04 Accessed online: www.statistics.gov.uk

National Statistics (ONS) (2004e) Client group analysis: quarterly bulletin – the population of working age on key benefits, February 2004 *National Statistics First Release* 16.6.04 Accessed online: www.dwp.gov.uk/asd/asd1/cga_wa/CGA_WA_Feb04_bulletin.pdf

National Statistics (ONS) (2004f) *Key Statistics for urban areas in England and Wales* Accessed online: www.statistics.gov.uk/downloads/census2001/ks_ua_ew_part2.pdf

Office of the Deputy Prime Minister (ODPM) (2003) *Sustainable Communities: Building for the future*

Olympic Coordinating Authority (OCA) (2002) *Annual Report 2001-2* Accessed online: www.gamesinfo.com.au/pdf/OCAAnnualReport_final.pdf

Olympic Games Study Commission (2003) *Report to the 115th IOC Session* Accessed online: www.multimedia.olympic.org/pdf/en_report_725.pdf

Preuss H (2000) *Economics of the Olympic Games: hosting the games 1972-2000* Walla Walla Press

PricewaterhouseCoopers (2002) *Business and Economic Benefits of the Sydney 2000 Olympic Games – a collation of evidence* Accessed online: www.gamesinfo.com.au/pi/ARPICOE.html

Rennie Short J (2003) Going for Gold: Globalising the Olympics, localising the Games *Research Bulletin 100A* Globalisation and World Cities Study Group and Network. Accessed online: www.lboro.ac.uk/gawc/rb/rb/100.html

Seager A (2004) Greeks are still hoping for gold *The Guardian* 30.8.04

Searle G (2002) Uncertain legacy: Sydney's Olympic stadiums *European Planning Studies* 10.7, 845-860

Sport England (no date) *Manchester 2002 The XVII Commonwealth Games: Wider opportunities programme* Sport England

Spring C (2003) *Taking a Sporting Chance: Regeneration and renewal* 6.6.03

Swann P (2001) *When Do Major Sporting Events Leave a Lasting Economic Legacy?* Accessed online: www.innovativeeconomics.org/games.htm

Sydney Morning Herald (2004) Games venues 'costing $46m a year' 29.7.04 Accessed online: www.rics.org/ricscms/bin/show?class=Feature&template=/includes/showfeature.html&id=1254

UK Sport (2004) *Measuring Success 2: The economic impact of major sports events* Accessed online: www.uksport.gov.uk/template.asp?id=1855

Waitt G (2003) Social impacts of the Sydney Olympics *Annals of Tourism Research* 30.1, 194-215

Washington Post (2004) *Athens readies itself for 2004 Summer Olympics* Accessed online: www.theseoultimes.com/ST/?url=/ST/db/read.php?idx=625

Yu M (2004) *The Economic and Social Impacts of Hosting Selected International Games* Research and Library Services Division Legislative Council Secretariat of the Hong Kong Government Accessed online: www.legco.gov.hk

Chapter 2

Arup (2002) *London Olympics 2012 – Costs and benefits* Final report summary Arup

Blair T (2004) London 2012 – a vision for the Olympic and Paralympic Games *Open letter* London 2012

Chaplin T (2004) Sports facilities as urban redevelopment catalysts: Baltimore's Camden Yards and Cleveland's Gateway *Journal of the American Planning Association* 70, 193-209

Cheshire P and Gordon I (1998) Territorial Competition: Some lessons for policy *Annals of Regional Science* 32.3, 321-346

Cochrane A (2003) 'The new urban policy: towards empowerment or incorporation? The practice of urban policy' in Imrie R and Raco M (eds) *Urban Renaissance? New Labour, community and urban policy* The Policy Press, 223-234

Cochrane A, Peck J and Tickell A (2002) 'Olympic dreams: Visions of partnership' in Peck J and Ward K (eds) *City of Revolution: Restructuring Manchester* Manchester University Press, 95-115

Delanty G (2004) *Community* Routledge

Dorling D and Thomas B (2004) *People and Places: A 2001 Census atlas of the UK* The Policy Press

The Economist (2004) London's Olympic spirit *The Economist* 20.5.04

English Heritage (2004) *A Welcome Home: A new sense of place for the Thames Gateway* English Heritage.

Essex S and Chalkley B (1998) Olympic Games: Catalyst of urban change *Leisure Studies* 17, 187-206

Hall T and Hubbard P (1998) *The Entrepreneurial City: Geographies of politics, regime, and representation* John Wiley

Harding A, Deas I, Evans R and Wilks-Heeg S (2004) 'Reinventing cities in a restructuring region? The rhetoric and reality of renaissance in Liverpool and Manchester' in Boddy M and Parkinson M (eds) *City Matters: Competitiveness, cohesion and urban governance* The Policy Press, 33-50

Healthcare Commission (2004) *The State of Healthcare Report 2004* Accessed online: www.healthcarecommission.org.uk

Hiller H (1988) 'Impact and image: the convergence of urban factors in preparing for the 1988 Calgary Winter Olympics' in Syme G, Shaw B, Fenton M and Mueller W (eds) *The Planning and Evaluation of Hallmark Events* Avebury, 119-131

Hughes R (2001) *Barcelona* The Harvill Press

Imrie R and Raco M (2003) 'Community and the changing nature of urban policy' in Imrie R and Raco M (eds) *Urban Renaissance? New Labour, community and urban policy* The Policy Press, 3-36

Imrie R and Thomas H (1995) Urban policy processes and the politics of urban regeneration *International Journal of Urban and Regional Research* 19, 479-494

Jones C (2001) A level playing field? Sports stadium infrastructure and urban development in the United Kingdom *Environment and Planning* A 33, 845-861

Lee P (2002) The economic and social justification for publicly financed stadia: The case of Vancouver's BC Place stadium *European Planning Studies* 10, 861-873

London 2012 (2004a) Response to the Questionnaire for Cities Applying to Become Candidate Cities to Host the Games of the XXX Olympiad and the Paralympic Games in 2012

London 2012 (2004b) *London 2012 – a vision for the Olympic Games and Paralympic Games*

Martinez A (2001) 'Countdown to the homeless Olympics' Accessed online: www.reportage.uts.edu.au/stories/2000/jun00/countdown.html

National Council of Voluntary Organisations (NCVO) (2004) Briefing on NCVO's Olympic Lottery Bill campaign *Briefing A1B18C115D1926*

Noll R and Zimblast A (1997) Sports, jobs and taxes – are new stadiums worth the cost? *The Brookings Review* 15, 35-39

PricewaterhouseCoopers (2001) *Business and Economic Benefits of the Sydney 2000 Olympics: a collation of evidence* Government of New South Wales

Raco M (2003) 'New Labour, community and the future of Britain's urban renaissance' in Imrie R and Raco M (eds) *Urban Renaissance? New Labour, community and urban policy* The Policy Press, 235-250

Rawnsley A (2003) We don't need this five-ring circus *The Observer* 19.1.03

Shapcott M (1998) 'Bread not circuses: response to Olds' Accessed online: www.divcom.otago.ac.nz

Smith H (2004) Greece facing decade of debt as Olympic bill soars *The Guardian* 16.6.04

Synadinos P (2001) 'Post-Olympic future: A picture of the future' Accessed online: www.olympic.org/upload/news/olympic_review/review_200219123748_uk.pdf

Turok I (1992) Property-led regeneration: panacea or placebo? *Environment and Planning* A 24, 361-379

Waitt G (1999) Playing games with Sydney: Marketing Sydney for the 2000 Olympics *Urban Studies* 36, 1055-1077

Weaver M (2002) What's the big deal in the end? *The Guardian* 7.7.02

Weaver M (2001) Housing row threatens pioneering regeneration project *The Guardian* 20.2.01

Chapter 3

Arup (2002) *London Olympics 2012 – costs and benefits* Final report summary

Australian Special Events Industry Newsletter (2002) 'Was Sydney the Best Games ever for Business?' Accessed online: www.specialevents.com.au/archiveprev/2002/02feb02/newsfeb02/games.html

Department of Social Security (1997) *Unemployment and Jobseeking* Report 62

ETC Research & Intelligence (2000) *Sightseeing in the UK 1999* Appendix 2, 86-87

Green D (2003) 'Olympics won't bring employment boom' Accessed online: www.policyalternatives.ca

Llewelyn-Davies with LSE (2000) *Regeneration Strategy for Park Royal* Llewelyn Davies

London Development Agency (2004) After the Gold Rush: Securing a sustainable employment legacy *Presentation by Syrus Bitaali, Institute for Public Policy Research* 17.6.04

National Statistics (ONS) (2004) *Indices of Deprivation for Wards in England, 2000* Accessed online: www.statistics.gov.uk/StatBase/Product.asp?vlnk=9421&Pos=1&ColRank=2&Rank=272

Office of the Deputy Prime Minister (ODPM) (2003) *Sustainable Communities: building for the future*

Olympic Coordinating Authority (OCA) (2002) *Annual Report 2001-2* Accessed online: www.gamesinfo.com.au/pdf/OCAAnnualReport_final.pdf

Robinson K (2003) London's Olympic Bid *Tourism* Autumn

Symanski S (2002a) *Winter Olympics – business suffers as locals flee* Creative Resistance British Columbia Accessed online: www.creativeresistance.ca

Szymanski S (2002b) The Economic Impact of the World Cup *World Economics* 3.1, 169-177

Thom G and Convery P (2003) 'Employer Engagement and the London Labour Market' Department for Work and Pensions *Research Report* 185 The Stationery Office

Williams G (2004) 'Lower Lea Valley – High hopes for Olympics' EP Newsletter Government Office for London

Chapter 5

Cashman R (2003) *Impact of the Games on Olympic Host Cities* Centre d'Estudis Olympics

Coalter F (1999) Sport and recreation in the UK: Flow with the flow or buck the trends? *Managing Leisure: An International Journal* 4.1, 24-39

Department for Culture, Media and Sport/Cabinet Office (DCMS/Cabinet Office) (2002) *Game Plan: A strategy for delivering Government's sport and physical activity objectives* Strategy Unit

Draper R (2003) Interview in *Sports Management* 7.3, 14-16

Hindson A, Gidlow B and Peebles C (1994) The 'trickle-down' effect of top-level sport: Myth or reality? A case study of the Olympics *Australian Leisure and Recreation* 4.1, 16-24

International Centre for Research and Consultancy for the Tourism and Hospitality Industries (ICRCTHI) (2003) *Sports Development Impact of the Commonwealth Games: study of volunteers (pre-games)* UK Sport

MORI (2004) *The Sports Development Impact of the Commonwealth Games 2002: Final report* Research Conducted for UK Sport in Greater Manchester, Blackburn, Congleton and Liverpool MORI

Payne W, Reynolds M, Brown S and Fleming A (2003) *Sports Role Models and their Impact on Participation in Physical Activity: A literature review* VicHealth Accessed online: www.vichealth.vic.gov.au

Ritchie JRB (2000) Turning 16 days into 16 years through Olympic legacies *Event Management* 6.11

Sport England (no date) *The Condition and Refurbishment of Public Sector Sports Facilities* Sport England

sportscotland (2004) Curling Success and its Impact on Participation *Research Report 92*

Veal AJ (2003) Tracking Change: Leisure participation and policy in Australia, 1985-2002 *Annals of Leisure Research* 6.3, 245-277

Waitt G (2001) The Olympic Spirit and Civic Boosterism: The Sydney 2000 Olympics *Tourism Geographies* 3.3, 249-278

Chapter 6

Bentley T (2004) *The Self-Creating Society* Demos

Department for Culture, Media and Sport (DCMS) (2001) *Culture and Creativity: The next ten years*

Frankland R(2000) *Media Briefing, Indigenous Unit – Australian Film Commission* Sydney Media Centre

Garcia B and Miah A (2000) *Olympic Ideals and Disney Dreams: Opportunities and constraints for cultural representation during Sydney's opening ceremony* Accessed online: www.humankinetics.com/products/hperd.cfm

Garcia B (2003) *Recommendations for the Programming, Management and Promotion of an Olympic Cultural Programme* University of Glasgow: Centre for Cultural Policy Research.

Garcia B (2002) 'The Concept of Olympic Cultural Programmes: Origins, evolution and projection' originally published in *Fundamental lessons about Olympic themes on-line* University of Barcelona: Centre for Olympic Studies

Hewison R and Holden J (2004) *The Right to Art* Demos

Leonard M (1997) *Britain TM* Demos.

Leonard M and Alakeson V (2000) *Going Public: Diplomacy for the information society* Foreign Policy Centre.

Leonard M and Small A (2003) *Norwegian Public Diplomacy* Foreign Policy Centre

Office for National Statistics (ONS) (2004) Key Statistics for Newham Accessed online: www.newham.info/research/Census2001/KSBorough/Table05.htm

Chapter 7

Barton D (2004) *Lasting Legacy* Accessed online: www.rfu.com

Bird W (forthcoming) *Can Green Space and Biodiversity Increase Levels of Physical Activity?* RSPB

Civil Aviation Authority (2004) Accessed online: www.caa.co.uk/docs/80/airport_data/200308/Table_12_1_Intl_Air_Pax_Traffic_Route_Analysis.csv

Department for Culture, Media and Sport/Cabinet Office (DCMS/Cabinet Office) (2002) *Game Plan: a strategy for delivering Government's sport and physical activity objectives* Strategy Unit

Department for Work and Pensions (DWP) (2004) *Building on New Deal: Local solutions meeting individual needs*

Grayling T (ed) (2001) *Any More Fares? Delivering better bus services* ippr

HM Treasury (HMT) (2004a) *2004 Spending Review: Public Service Agreements 2005-2008* Accessed online: www.hm-treasury.gov.uk/spending_review/spend_sr04/psa/spend_sr04_psaindex.cfm

HM Treasury (HMT) (2004b) *Russell Commission on a National Youth Volunteering Strategy* Accessed online: www.hm-treasury.gov.uk/media/A1866/russell_commission04_24.pdf

Jobcentre Plus (2003) *Jobcentre Plus Vision*

Northern Ireland Government Departments (NIGD) (2002) *Priorities and Budget: 2004-2006* Accessed online: www.pfgni.gov.uk/pab04.pdf

Office of the Deputy Prime Minister and Department for Environment, Food and Rural Affairs (ODPM and DEFRA) (2004a?) *Creating Sustainable Communities: Greening the Gateway. A greenspace strategy for Thames Gateway*

Office of the Deputy Prime Minister and Sport England (ODPM and Sport England) (2004b) 'Sport and Regeneration Team Up for a Healthier Future' Rooker News Release 2004/0139 17.6.04 Accessed online: www.odpm.gov.uk/pns/DisplayPN.cgi?pn_id=2004_0139

Robinson P (forthcoming) 'Achieving full employment' in Pearce N and Paxton W (eds) *Rethinking Social Justice* Methuen

Rowe N and Moore S (2004) *Research Briefing Note: Participation in sport – results from the General Household Survey 2002* Sport England

Rugby Football Union (RFU) (2003) *Rugby – making an impact RFU Action Plan*

Sport England (2004a) *Driving up Participation: The challenge for sport*

Sport England (2004b) *The Framework for Sport in England – Making England an active and successful sporting nation: a vision for 2020*

Sports Council for Wales (2004) *The Sports Council for Wales: The vision* Accessed online: www.sports-council-wales.co.uk/ organisation.cfm?main_nav=about_us&sub_nav=organisation

Stanley K (2004) *Something for Something: A national youth action programme* ippr

Appendix 1
Existing or potential programmes in the Olympic boroughs

New Deal for Communities
Partnerships (of local people, community and voluntary organisations, public agencies, local authorities and business) generally expected to focus on the following five themes: worklessness; crime, the fear of crime, and community safety; health; housing and the physical environment; educational achievement.

Neighbourhood Renewal Fund
Available to eighty eight most deprived local authorities in England. The fund must be spent on tackling deprivation and the implementation of Local Neighbourhood Renewal Strategies to help the main public sector service providers and others think about how services could better meet the needs of people in deprived neighbourhoods. It is the responsibility of LSPs to make decisions on how the NRF is spent.

Local Strategic Partnerships
Partnerships of senior public, private and voluntary and community sector representatives that: deliver better services to local people especially those living in the most deprived neighbourhoods; develop and deliver a community strategy which provides a framework for other strategies in the borough; develop and deliver a local neighbourhood renewal strategy; make decisions on how the NRF is spent.

Employment Zones
To allow jobseekers to benefit from the expertise of the public as well as private sector.

Community Chest and Community Learning Chest (CLC)
The Neighbourhood Renewal Community Chest (NRCC) and CLC are two of three 'Community Participation Programmes' designed to help community and voluntary sector groups play a more active and influential role in delivering the objectives of Neighbourhood Renewal in their areas.

Community Empowerment Fund (CEF)
The CEF is the other 'Community Participation Programme'. The main purpose of the CEF is to support the development of a 'Community Empowerment Network' (CEN). An important element of the work of CENs is making connections with small, marginalised groups and individuals, particularly those based in the most deprived areas and estates, who have not had much say in the past about decisions that affect their lives. This is a constant process as populations are always changing.

Community Development Venture Fund
Venture capital investment for both economic and social gain in businesses in under-invested communities. It is different from investment in social and community enterprises that do not aim to generate sufficient revenue or profit.

Active Community Unit Experience Corps Scheme
Launched in November 2001 with a mission to recruit within three years 250,000 over-fifty year olds that wished and were able to give some of their time to work voluntarily in their local community.

Pilot Clear Zones
Helps create liveable, accessible and lively urban centres where traffic congestion, pollution, noise, stress and the other negative effects of mobility are eliminated or reduced.

Sport Action Zones
A proactive initiative to create an effective and sustainable sporting infrastructure in areas of high social and economic deprivation and ensure there is a more equitable participation in sport. Communities which suffer from the effects of poverty and deprivation have been consistently shown to have lower levels of participation in sport and recreation than those more advantaged areas. Residents within deprived areas are often excluded from mainstream sport through a host of inter-linked economic, social and physical factors, such as the costs of using facilities, poor access to transport, lack of confidence and low self esteem.

Note: The last two initiatives in the table – 'Pilot Clear Zones' and 'Sport Action Zones' – are not currently running within the Olympic boroughs but are interesting examples that could both use the Olympics to deliver on their own objectives whilst at the same time contributing towards a sustainable Olympic legacy.

Appendix 2
A note on Methodology

In the course of our research we held five seminars, each on an individual legacy theme. There were over 150 attendees. At each seminar a representative from London 2012 (or at the employment seminar, the London Development Agency) presented the Bid Team's latest legacy thinking before an expert responded. There followed a round table discussion of relevant stakeholders (representatives of government, academia and community groups for example). The experts reflected some of this discussion in the chapters they have contributed here.

As well as the seminars, we spoke to a range of stakeholders in the London 2012 bid and a number of people involved in the Sydney Olympic Games and Manchester Commonwealth Games. They are listed below.

Jeff Angel	Total Environment Centre, Sydney
Jerry Bingham	UK Sport
Paul Brickell	Leaside Regeneration
Chris Brown	Igloo Regeneration
James Bulley	London 2012
Terry Burwell	Rugby Football Union
Hugh Carr-Harris	London Remade
Richard Cope	Environment Agency
Frances Done	Audit Commission
Trevor Dorling	London Borough of Greenwich
Kate Egford	Sport England North West
Kate Foley	Renaisi
Dan Fox	Engineering and Technology Board
Beatriz Garcia	Centre for Cultural Policy Research, University of Glasgow

Lesley Giddins	David Taylor Partners; ex-Director of 2002 Manchester Commonwealth Games SRB programme
Michael Knight	New South Wales Olympics Minister and President, Sydney Organising Committee of the Olympic Games
Kevin Kumar	London Metropolitan University
Neil Lawson and Andrew Crossley	The East London Community Organisation (TELCO)
Andrew Mawson	Community Action Network
Sean McGonigle and John Adan	New East Manchester New Deal for the Community
Rob McVeigh	Sydney Lawyer
Steve Moffit	Creative Partnerships East London
Lynn Pegler	British Waterways
Sheldon Phillips	Head of Marketing Partnerships, North West Development Agency
David Powell	David Powell Associates
David Richmond	General, Sydney Organising Committee of the Olympic Games
Vicky Rosin	Libraries and Theatres Department, Manchester City Council; ex-Head of Manchester City Council Commonwealth Games Unit
Tanya Ross	Buro Happold
Nick Rowley	No. 10 Downing Street; ex-Adviser to New South Wales Premier
Carol Souter	Heritage Lottery Fund
Sarah Tebbutt	Her Majesty's Treasury
Geoff Thompson	Youth Charter for Sport, Culture and the Arts
Ian Tuckett	Coin Street Community Builders
Richard Yule	English Table Tennis Association
Colin Zetie	Groundwork East London